MUSIC THEORY

FROM **KEYS AND SCALES**
TO **RHYTHM AND MELODY,**
AN ESSENTIAL PRIMER ON THE
BASICS OF MUSIC THEORY

101

BRIAN BOONE and MARC SCHONBRUN

ADAMS MEDIA
NEW YORK   LONDON   TORONTO   SYDNEY   NEW DELHI

Adams media

Adams Media
An Imprint of Simon & Schuster, Inc.
100 Technology Center Drive
Stoughton, MA 02072

Copyright © 2017 by Simon & Schuster, Inc.

All rights reserved, including the right to reproduce this book or portions thereof in any form whatsoever. For information address Adams Media Subsidiary Rights Department, 1230 Avenue of the Americas, New York, NY 10020.

First Adams Media hardcover edition
AUGUST 2017

11 2023

Library of Congress Cataloging-in-Publication Data
Boone, Brian, author. | Schonbrun, Marc, author.
Music theory 101 / Brian Boone and Marc Schonbrun.
Avon, Massachusetts: Adams Media, 2017.
Series: 101
Includes index.
LCCN 2017015056 (print) | LCCN 2017017218 (ebook) | ISBN 9781507203668 (hc) | ISBN 9781507203675 (ebook)
LCSH: Music theory--Elementary works.
LCC MT7 (ebook) | LCC MT7 .B693 2017 (print) | DDC 781--dc23
LC record available at https://lccn.loc.gov/2017015056

ISBN 978-1-5072-0366-8
ISBN 978-1-5072-0367-5 (ebook)

ADAMS MEDIA and colophon are trademarks of Simon and Schuster.

For information about special discounts for bulk purchases, please contact Simon & Schuster Special Sales at 1-866-506-1949 or business@simonandschuster.com.

The Simon & Schuster Speakers Bureau can bring authors to your live event. For more information or to book an event contact the Simon & Schuster Speakers Bureau at 1-866-248-3049 or visit our website at www.simonspeakers.com.

Interior design by Colleen Cunningham

Manufactured in the United States of America

Many of the designations used by manufacturers and sellers to distinguish their products are claimed as trademarks. Where those designations appear in this book and Simon & Schuster, Inc., was aware of a trademark claim, the designations have been printed with initial capital letters.

Contains material adapted from the following titles published by Adams Media, an Imprint of Simon & Schuster, Inc.: *The Everything® Music Theory Book, 2nd Edition* by Marc Schonbrun, copyright © 2011, ISBN 978-1-4405-1182-0 and *The Everything® Reading Music Book* by Marc Schonbrun, copyright © 2005, ISBN 978-1-59337-324-5.

CONTENTS

CHAPTER 4: MUSICAL KEYS AND KEY SIGNATURES 71

CHAPTER 5: MODES AND OTHER SCALES 87

CHAPTER 6: CHORDS 103

CHAPTER 7: CHORD INVERSIONS AND PROGRESSIONS 129

CHAPTER 8: EXPLORING HARMONY 151

CHAPTER 9: READING MUSIC 181

CHAPTER 10: EXPRESSION MARKINGS
AND OTHER SYMBOLS 197

CHAPTER 11: APPLYING MUSICAL THEORY KNOWLEDGE 217

FINAL EXAM: ANALYZING A PIECE OF MUSIC 237

INDEX 245

INTRODUCTION

Music theory is the study of music itself—it attempts to decipher why the patterns in music are what they are and how that in turn makes music work. Music is, after all, a highly intricate and structured art form that involves a great deal of math, science, and acoustics. And it's true that understanding music takes time and effort. But learning more about the music you love doesn't have to be a challenge! This guide will help you master the tools you need to read, play, and comprehend music.

This book is different from other books on music theory that you may have bought. Many theory books cater to the experienced musician and are filled with complex terms and assumptions that can overwhelm the everyday reader. These books also tend to focus on classical music and often ignore other types of music. In comparison, *Music Theory 101* presents the topic in a clear, easy-to-understand fashion that encompasses many musical genres and instruments.

Whether you play music or just want to know more about it, this book will help you understand how music works and how all its elements fit together. Music theory takes the *sounds* of music and translates them into *words*; it takes a look at how music has evolved over the years and explores what we can learn from those changes.

This book covers the essential aspects you need to know, such as:

- How to understand rhythm and time signatures
- How chords and scales are constructed
- How to write and understand traditional harmony

- How to identify keys and how keys are organized
- How to understand articulations and ornaments on written music
- How to use modes to expand harmony

Music theory doesn't have to be confusing or overly complicated. And while it can be true that learning music theory is not an easy task, this book will lead you through the process with confidence and clarity. So let's explore (and demystify) the fascinating world of music theory.

Note: In addition to examples in standard music notation, you'll also see guitar tablature included in many of the figures as well as guitar chord diagrams. If you play guitar, you'll be able to play along with many of the examples included in this book and strum along with the harmonies to help you learn.

Chapter 1

The Basics of Music

Whether you are new to the study of music or are adept at reading and playing music, you need to have a firm grasp of the basics and an appreciation of its rich compositional history to understand music theory. With that in mind, this chapter offers an overview of the basic musical terms and concepts upon which music theory is built, as well as a brief history of musical styles.

THE PERIODS OF "CLASSICAL" MUSIC

A History of Styles

While there are more genres of music than we've got space to write them down, not to mention the subgenres of all of those, there are essentially a few overarching styles under which most music can be categorized. While all more or less follow the rules and structures of Western music theory, the following types of music also boast their own highly recognizable and innovative tropes, details, and traditions. Here's a brief history of symphonic and orchestral musical styles.

BAROQUE (C. 1600–1760)

Baroque music is complex, soaring, heavily ornamented, and undeniably grand, and is the basis for the classical and symphonic music that followed. The baroque period produced some of the most groundbreaking composers, including Johann Sebastian Bach, Antonio Vivaldi, and George Handel.

CLASSICAL (C. 1760–1820)

While you often hear the term *classical* in reference to any kind of music that involves a large group of varied instruments playing a complex, lyrics-free composition, the term is more accurately applied to a certain period in European music. And while "classical" music seems fancy and grand, classical composers actually tried to strip down music to its basic and most beautiful elements in favor of clear, strong melodies. Some of the best-known composers come from the classical period, such as Wolfgang Amadeus Mozart, Ludwig van Beethoven, and Franz Joseph Haydn.

ROMANTIC (C. 1780–1900)

In the romantic era, composers attempted to evoke particular feelings and even tell stories with emotional and slightly informal pieces. They idealized nature, love, spirituality, and foreign lands in a style similar to other storytelling forms, such as opera and ballet. Major romantic composers include Johannes Brahms, Pyotr Ilyich Tchaikovsky (a.k.a. Peter Ilich Tchaikovsky), and Richard Wagner.

MODERN (C. 1900–1975)

With musical traditions going back hundreds of years, one option for modern composers was to reject history, and its rules, and instead experiment. Consistent and pleasant melody, harmony, and rhythm was often downplayed in favor of dissonance, heavy use of minor keys, strange meter, and even random sounds. Some of the notable composers who shook things up during this period include Richard Strauss, Claude Debussy, Igor Stravinsky, and Erik Satie.

Notable

Western music grew from European musical traditions. Those traditions started with the simple *monophonic* (or one-voice) chants used as a form of worship by monks. This was the most common type of music from about 350–1050, which means it took a good 700 years for *polyphonic* liturgical music (multiple voices singing different lines at the same time) to develop. Polyphonic music dominated from about 1050–1300, until more complex compositions and instrumentations began to emerge.

CONTEMPORARY SYMPHONIC MUSIC
(C. 1975–PRESENT)

The history rejected by modernist composers has come full circle, with many musicians looking to the golden ages of the seventeenth and eighteenth centuries for inspiration and creating lush, textured, melody-driven symphonies. Other composers have continued to experiment with music, taking it to the very edge of logic and what could reasonably be called music, carrying on the avant-garde work of the early twentieth century. There's also been a movement toward minimalism. Influenced by rock-and-roll, minimalists favor sparse instrumentation to deliver short melodies that repeat and grow in complexity. Major names in the last forty years of composition include Philip Glass, John Adams, and Thomas Adès.

Notable

All the music described in the previous section is Western, meaning that it stems from what's historically been called the West: Europe and later, the Americas. Asia, Africa, the Americas, and indigenous peoples throughout the world each have their own rich musical histories—all of which can and have filled their own books. This book focuses almost entirely on the forms and systems of Western music.

TERMS TO KNOW

Music Piece by Piece

Music theory explores what has been done in other music in order to reach a greater overall understanding. Since you will see the language of written music throughout this book, you must be able to read it. You will need to read in multiple clefs, since standard notation uses treble and bass clefs at a minimum and often throws in alto clef too. Here is a basic review to help you make sense of what you are reading. There is also a somewhat detailed review of rhythms because it can be a difficult concept to understand; even if you know how to decipher the notes on a staff, you may still be uneasy with the counting aspect. If this chapter is already scaring you, you can get a brief tutorial on reading music in Chapters 9 and 10 of this book or you might want to pick up a book strictly on reading music and keep it around; it will help you greatly in understanding this material!

NOTES

What better place to start than with notes? Here's a short sample of music; try to dissect what's going on and see if you have all the information you need.

As you can see from this figure, this is a short excerpt from a piece of solo piano music. Here is what you are seeing:

1. There are notes placed on two musical staffs: one treble staff and one bass staff.
2. The staffs are further defined by their clefs.
3. The notes are identified only by use of a clef; otherwise, they are simply dots sitting on lines and spaces.

If you want to talk about the notes, you have to talk about clefs because clefs actually define the name of the notes in a staff.

CLEFS

A clef is a symbol that sits at the beginning of every staff of music. A staff contains five lines and four spaces. How do you know where the note A or the note C is? The missing element is the clef, which defines what notes go where and functions a lot like a map. Placing a treble clef at the start of the staff defines the lines and spaces with note names. The following figure shows the notes of a treble staff.

The treble clef circles around the note G. This is why it's commonly called the G clef. As for the notes, there is an important pattern. Look at the lowest line, which is designated E. Follow the musical alphabet to find where the next note is. The F is in the space just above the E. The staff ascends in this fashion—line, then space, then line—as it cycles through the musical alphabet (A-B-C-D-E-F-G).

The bass clef is a different clef than the treble and identifies not only different note names but also notes in different ranges. The bass clef is used for instruments that have a lower pitch, like a bass guitar. Even though the bass clef sits on the same five-line staff, it defines very different notes. Many musicians can read treble clef because it is the most common clef. It is more difficult, however, for many musicians to read bass clef. In order to make progress in understanding theory, you will need to be adept at reading all clefs. The next figure shows the notes of a bass clef staff.

E F G A B C D E F G A B C

Notable

Even though you may understand the notes on both clefs, the only way to become proficient is to read other clefs as often as you can. Set aside a few minutes each day to look at other clefs so you can easily identify their notes. Since clefs define notes, think of being able to read in many clefs as a kind of musical literacy.

GRAND STAFF AND MIDDLE C

Grouping the bass clef and the treble clef together creates the grand staff. The grand staff is used in piano writing. To make a grand staff, connect a treble and a bass staff, or clef, with a brace, as shown in the following figure.

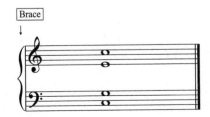

Brace

The grand staff reveals a very important note: middle C. The following figure shows a middle C.

When you look at the previous figure, can you tell whether the note belongs to the bass clef or the treble clef? Actually, it belongs equally to both. If you trace down from the treble clef, one ledger line below the staff is a C. If you look at the bass clef notes, one ledger line above the staff is also a C. They are, in fact, the same pitch on the piano. This note is called middle C because it's right in the middle of everything. Middle C will come up throughout this book, so keep track of it!

MOVABLE C CLEFS

The last type of clef is the C clef. Typically this clef is associated with the viola because it's the most common instrument that reads in C clef; however, other instruments read it as well. When the C clef is used with the viola, it is called the alto clef. Thankfully, this clef is very easy to read; the symbol for the C clef has two semicircles that curve into the middle of the staff and basically point toward the middle line, which is a C—and it's not just any C, it's middle C. The next figure shows the notes for alto clef.

D E F G A B C D E F G A B

Since this is a movable clef, you can place the clef anywhere you want; whatever lines the two semicircles point to become middle C. Some very old choral music uses a different movable C clef for each part (tenor clef, alto clef, and soprano clef). As long as you know that the clef always points toward middle C, you will be able to decipher the notes in this clef.

Notable

When notes use ledger lines that are extremely high or extremely low, they can be difficult to read; it's much easier to read notes that sit in the staff you are reading. Using different clefs allows you to move the location of middle C so that the majority of your notes are in and around the staff.

ACCIDENTALS

Notes can be altered with the use of accidentals. If you've heard of B-flat (B♭) or C-sharp (C♯), then you've heard of an accidental. Accidentals are used to raise and lower the pitch of a tone. There are two types of accidentals: single and double.

- A single accidental is the common ♭ and ♯ symbol.
- A ♭ lowers the pitch by one half step.
- A ♯ raises a pitch by one half step.
- A ♮ (natural) cancels an accidental (either in a measure or from the given key signature).

In addition to the simple sharp and flat symbols, you will also see double accidentals.

- A ♭♭ lowers the pitch by two half steps.
- A ✕ raises a pitch by two half steps.
- A ♮ cancels the double accidental in the same way it cancels the single accidentals.

TIME

Gimmie a Beat

Time is a fundamental aspect of music theory that is often left out of formal music-theory study. Time is more than just counting beats and bars. Time can dictate the feel and flow of a piece; even harmony has a rhythm to it, aptly called harmonic rhythm. You'll start with time signatures, as they are the first time-related aspect you need to understand in detail.

TIME SIGNATURES

Music is divided into bars, or measures, for reading convenience and for musical purposes. Most music adheres to a meter, which affects the phrasing of the melody. If you don't have a lot of experience reading music, rhythm can be a very difficult concept to grasp.

Notable

A beat is a way of counting time when playing music. Beats are grouped together in a measure (the notes and rests that correspond to a certain number of beats). The grouping of strong and weak beats is called meter. You can find the meter signature (also called the time signature) at the beginning of every piece of music.

The most standard time signature is $\frac{4}{4}$ time, which is also called common time and is abbreviated by this symbol: **C**. Common time looks like a fraction and signifies two things. First, the top number 4 means that every measure will have four beats in it. The bottom number 4 indicates what note value will receive the beat; in this case, 4 stands for a quarter note (♩). So common time breaks up each measure into four beats, as a quarter note receives one beat. You can, of course, further divide the measure into as many small parts as you like, but in the end, it must still add up to four beats.

RHYTHM

Music is composed of pitch and rhythm. Although finer elements come into play later on, such as dynamics and expression, music can be made simply by knowing which note and how long to hold it. Without rhythm, people couldn't fully read music.

Rhythm is music's way of setting the duration of a note. Music accomplishes this task by varying the appearance of the notes that sit on the staff. Different rhythms indicate different note lengths. To get rolling, you need to hear about an essential concept: beat. Have you ever been to a concert and clapped along with 30,000 other fans? Have you noticed how everyone claps together in a steady pattern? Did you ever wonder how 30,000 people could possibly agree on anything? If you've been to a dance club, you may have noticed that there is always a steady drumbeat or bass line, usually up-tempo, to drive the music along. Those are examples of pulse and beat in music. Rhythm is a primal element, and pulse and beat are universal concepts.

BASIC RHYTHMS

You Have to Start Somewhere

In music, changing the appearance of the notes indicates the rhythm. Remember, the location of the notes is fixed on the staff and will never change. However, the note's appearance varies, indicating how long that note should be held. Now, here are the basic musical symbols for rhythm.

QUARTER NOTES

A quarter note (♩) is signified with a filled-in black circle (also called a notehead) and a stem. It is the simplest rhythm to discuss. Quarter notes receive one count; their duration is one beat (see the following figure).

Quarter Notes

HALF NOTES

The next in our series of simple rhythms is the half note (♩). As you can see, the half note looks similar to the quarter note, except the circle is not filled in. Like a quarter note, the half note has a single stem that points either up or down. The half note receives two counts; its duration is two beats. In relation to the quarter note, the half note is twice as long because it receives two counts (see the next figure).

Half Notes

WHOLE NOTES

A whole note (o) is a rhythm that receives four beats. It's twice as long as a half note and four times as long as a quarter note—count to yourself: one, two, three, four. A whole note is represented as an open circle without a stem. It is probably the single longest rhythmic value that you will come across. Whole notes are easy to spot because they are the only notes that lack a stem (see the following figure).

Whole Notes

EIGHTH NOTES

The smallest rhythm you have encountered thus far is the quarter note, which lasts for one beat. Dividing this beat further allows musicians to explore faster rhythms and faster passages. Chopping the quarter note in half gives us the eighth note (♪), which receives half of one beat (see the next figure).

Eighth Notes

SIXTEENTH NOTES

The beat can be broken down even further for the faster note values. The next rhythm is the sixteenth note (♬), which breaks the quarter note into four equal parts and the eighth note into two equal parts (see the following figure).

FASTER NOTE VALUES

It's possible to keep chopping the beat into smaller and smaller parts. The next step beyond sixteenth notes is the thirty-second note, which breaks one beat into eight equal parts. Just like the transition from eighth to sixteenth notes, going from sixteenth to thirty-second notes will add another flag or beam to the notes. Add another flag and it will simply make the note value half the length of the previous note. The next figure shows faster note values.

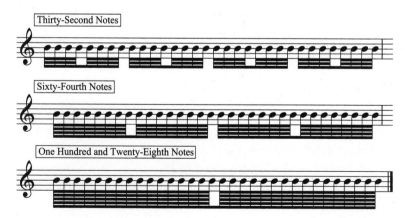

AUGMENTATION DOTS

You have focused on making note values smaller and smaller, but you can also make them larger by using an augmentation dot. Placing a small dot directly to the right of any note increases its duration by one-half. For example, placing a dot after a half note makes the dotted half last for three beats. The original half note receives two beats and the dot adds half the value of the original note (a half note): The dot adds one extra beat (a quarter note), bringing the total up to three beats. Any note can be dotted. The following figure is a chart of dotted rhythms and their duration.

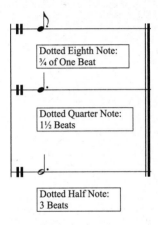

Dotted Eighth Note:
¾ of One Beat

Dotted Quarter Note:
1½ Beats

Dotted Half Note:
3 Beats

Notable

A dot extends the value of a note. A tie also extends notes. Both do the same thing, but visually, they do it differently. A dot added to a note requires that you figure out what half of the note value is and count it. A tie is sometimes easier to read because the notes are visually glued together.

TUPLETS

Up to this point, rhythms have been based on equal divisions of two. For example, breaking a whole note in half results in two half notes. In the same way, dividing a half note in two results in two quarter notes. As the divisions get smaller, going through eighth and sixteenth notes, the notes are continuously broken in half equally. However, beats can also be broken into other groupings—most importantly, groupings based on odd numbers such as three. Such odd groupings are commonly referred to as tuplets.

When you break a beat into three parts, you give birth to a triplet. The most basic triplet is the eighth-note triplet. An eighth-note triplet is simply three eighth notes that equally divide one beat into three parts (see the next figure). You could also look at it like a ratio: three notes equally divided in the same space as one beat. Since there are three notes in each beat, eighth-note triplets are faster than two eighth notes taking up the same beat. The more notes per beat, the faster they progress.

Tuplets don't have to be in threes, although that is the most common tuplet in music. You can have tuplets that divide a beat into any number of parts: five, seven, even eleven. The number above the grouping of notes indicates how it's supposed to be divided.

RESTS

All this talk about notes and rhythms wouldn't be complete without some discussion of rests. Everything you've learned about rhythms also applies to rests. The only difference is that a rest tells you not to do anything!

Every pitch needs duration. Rhythm defines how long notes should be sustained. Music isn't always about sound—rests are as common as pitches. Rests indicate a spot in the music where you don't play a sound. Since a rest does not have a pitch associated with it, it requires a different symbol. Here's a chart of the rests (see the following figure) and their associated notes.

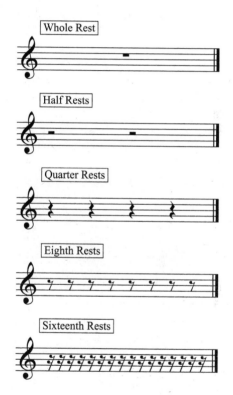

METER

Breaking Up the Beat

The last thing to explain is meter. You encountered one meter at the beginning of this chapter: common time, or $\frac{4}{4}$ meter. Now take a bit of time and look at the different meters.

SIMPLE METER

A simple meter is any meter that breaks up the beat into even divisions. This means that whatever the beat is—whether it's $\frac{4}{4}$, $\frac{3}{4}$, or $\frac{2}{4}$—each beat (which is a quarter note) is equally divided. The beat is broken into even divisions of two (eighth notes), four (sixteenth notes), or eight (thirty-second notes). (See the following examples of simple meter.)

What sets a simple meter apart from other meters is how the beats are grouped. The clearest way to see the groupings is through the use of eighth and sixteenth notes. Since the flags join and are visually grouped together, you can easily see how the notes and the beats break down. In a simple meter, you place slight natural accents on the strong beats, which are always on the first note of any rhythmic grouping. Whenever notes are grouped in twos or fours, you are in simple time. Since $\frac{4}{4}$, $\frac{3}{4}$, and $\frac{2}{4}$ are the most common meters and are all in simple time, you will become a pro at simple meters in short order!

COMPOUND METER

Simple meters have one important feature: groupings of two or four notes. The next meters are compound meters, which are broken into groups of three. This is what makes compound time different from simple time. Common compound meters are $\frac{3}{8}$, $\frac{6}{8}$, $\frac{9}{8}$, and $\frac{12}{8}$. Compound meters usually have an 8 in the lower part of the meter because the meter is based on eighth notes receiving the beat. (See the following examples.)

Notable

Compound time relies on groupings of three notes, so you need to adjust how you view beat durations. A click on the metronome does not always signify a quarter note. What it does signify is the pulse of the music. In common time, that click could be a dotted quarter note, so keep your concept of time elastic.

The previous figure illustrates the three-note groupings of compound meters. That is, $\frac{3}{8}$ simply contains one grouping of three, $\frac{6}{8}$ two groupings of three, and so on. Counting in $\frac{4}{4}$ and other simple meters hasn't been such a big deal. Simply set your metronome or tap your foot along with the quarter notes. In compound time, your beat becomes a grouping of three notes—more specifically, a grouping of three eighth notes (although if you were in $\frac{3}{16}$, three sixteenth notes would get the beat, but since time is all relative, it all works out the same).

The combination of simple and compound time signatures will get you through most music you'll encounter. Even so, composers and musicians love to stretch the boundaries. All the meters you've learned about so far have been divided into easy groupings. Other music exists in unusual groupings, called odd time.

Odd time or an odd meter is a meter that is asymmetric or has uneven groupings. Odd time can be expressed whenever 5, 7, 10, 11, 13, and 15 are the top value in a time signature. The bottom of the signature can be any rhythmic value; the top number determines if it's symmetric (simple) or asymmetric (odd) time. Take a look at a basic odd meter such as $\frac{5}{4}$ in the next figure.

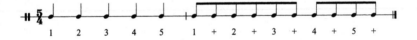

Chapter 2

Intervals

The most elemental part of music theory is to understand the relationships between single notes. The distance between those notes is an interval, which will serve as the foundation for practically every concept that you will explore throughout this book. Understanding intervals is extremely important.

INTERVALS

Going the Distance

Defined as the distance from one note to another, intervals provide the basic framework for everything else in music. Small intervals combine to form scales. Larger intervals combine to form chords. Intervals aid in voice leading, composition, and transposition. There are virtually no musical situations that don't use intervals (barring snare drum solos). Even in some of the extremely dissonant music of the twentieth century, intervals are still the basis for most composition and analysis.

There are five different types of intervals:

1. Major intervals
2. Minor intervals
3. Perfect intervals
4. Augmented intervals
5. Diminished intervals

You will learn all about the five types of intervals in this chapter, but before you go any further, you need a visual helper: the piano keyboard. Intervals can seem like an abstract concept; having some visual relationships to reference can make the concept more concrete and easier to grasp. The following figure shows the piano keyboard.

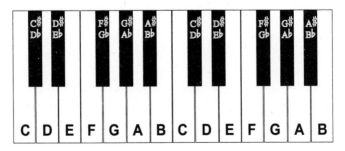

The keyboard shows you the location of all the notes within one full octave. It also shows you all the sharps and flats on the black keys.

Notable

Notice how C♯ and D♭ occupy the same key. This situation, in which one key can have more than one name, is called an enharmonic. This occurs on all black keys. The white keys have only one name, whereas the black keys always have a second possibility. (You'll learn more about that later in this book.)

HALF STEPS

The first interval to look at is the half step. It is the smallest interval that Western music uses (Eastern music uses quarter tones, which are smaller than a half step), and it's the smallest interval you can play on the majority of musical instruments. How far is a half step? Well, if you look at a piece of music, a great example of a half step is the distance from C to C♯ or D♭—remember that C♯ and D♭ sound the same. The next figure shows the half step in a treble staff.

Half Step

Now that you have been given a rudimentary explanation of a half step, go back to the piano. Stated simply, the piano is laid out in successive half steps starting from C. To get to the next available note, you simply progress to the next available key. If you are on a white key such as C, for example, the next note is the black key of C♯/D♭. You have moved a half step. Move from the black key to the white key of D and you've moved another half step. When you've done this twelve times, you have come back around to C and completed an octave, which is another interval.

Now, this is not always a steadfast rule. It is not always the case that you will move from a white key to a black key, or vice versa, in order to move a half step.

As you can see in the next figure, the movement between E and F and the movement between B and C are both carried out from white key to white key, with no black key between them. This means that B and C, and E and F, are a half step apart. This is called a natural half step, and it is the only exception to our half-step logic. The good news is that if you keep this in mind, all intervals will be much easier to define, not just half steps.

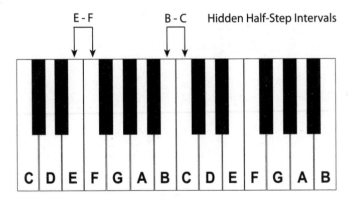

Why is there a half step between B and C and E and F when everywhere else it takes a whole step to get to the next letter name? The answer is simpler than you think. The sound of the C major scale (C–D–E–F–G–A–B–C) came first. The scale happened to have a half step between E and F and B and C. When the system of music was broken down and actually defined, that scale was laid out in white keys and had to fit the other half steps between the other notes. It really is arbitrary and provides another argument for the fact that sounds come first and then they are named or explained.

WHOLE STEPS

A whole step is simply the distance of two half steps combined. Movements from C to D or F♯ to G♯ are examples of whole steps. If you are getting the hang of both whole and half steps, you can take this information a bit further. You could skip to scales, which would, in turn, lead you to chords.

The intervals between E and F and B and C are still natural half steps. The next figure gives an example.

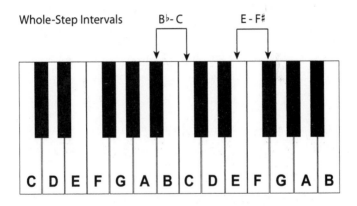

A whole step from E ends up on F♯ because you have to go two half steps to get to F♯, passing right by F♮. The same holds true for B♭ to C.

Now that you have gone through half and whole steps, the next step is the C major scale to see some of the other intervals out there.

INTERVALS FROM SCALES

The Easiest Way to See Intervals

You may be wondering why a discussion of the C major scale appears in the interval chapter. Simply put, once you know whole and half steps, you can spell any scale, but more important, the other intervals are much easier to see and learn through the use of a scale.

Notable

Usually when musicians name a large interval, they don't count the numbers of half steps they need to figure out the answer. They are so familiar with scales that they use that information to solve their puzzle. Scales are such useful bits of information, and they are, of course, made up of simple intervals!

INTERVALS IN THE C MAJOR SCALE

Forming a C major scale is pretty simple: You start and end on C, use every note in the musical alphabet, and don't use sharps or flats. The C major scale is easy to spell and understand because it doesn't contain sharps or flats. It's the scale you get if you play from C to C on just the white keys of a piano. The following figure shows the scale.

The distance between any two adjacent notes in the scale is simply a collection of half and whole steps. Now try skipping around the scale and see what intervals you come up with. Start with C as a basis for your work. Every interval will be the distance from C to some other note in the C scale.

To start, measure the distance where there is no distance at all. An interval of no distance is called unison. See the next figure.

Perfect Unison

Unison is more important than you think. While you won't see it in a solo piano score—you couldn't play the same key twice at the same time—when you learn to analyze a full score of music, it's handy to be able to tell when instruments are playing exactly the same notes rather than other intervals, such as octaves.

The movement from C to D is a whole step, but the interval is more formally called a major second. Every major second comprises two half steps' distance. See the next figure.

Major Second

The next interval is from C to E, which is four half steps' distance. It is called a major third (see the following figure).

Major Third

Next up is the distance from C to F, which is five half steps. It is called a perfect fourth, as seen in the next figure.

Perfect Fourth

Perfect fourth? Are you confused yet with the naming of these intervals? Hang in there! Before you get to why this is so, finish the scale. You have only begun to chip away at intervals.

The next interval is the distance from C to G. It is seven half steps and is called a perfect fifth (see the following figure).

Perfect Fifth

The interval from C to A, which is nine half steps, is called a major sixth. The next figure presents a major sixth.

Major Sixth

The next interval, from C to B, is eleven half steps. It is called a major seventh (see the following figure).

Major Seventh

To complete this scale, the last interval will be C to C. This interval is a distance of twelve half steps, or an octave (see the next figure).

Perfect Octave

INTERVALS IN THE C MINOR SCALE

Now that you've seen the intervals in the C major scale, here is the whole C minor scale and all its intervals. Look at the figure. What do you see?

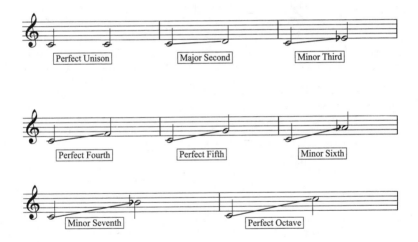

For starters, the third, sixth, and seventh intervals are now minor. That makes sense because those are the three notes that are different when you compare a C major and a C minor scale side by side, as in the next figure.

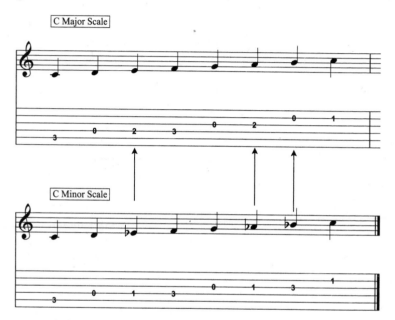

Only the 3rd, 6th and 7th change.

The intervals that were perfect in the major scale remain the same between both scales. However, the second note of the scale (C to D) remains the same in both scales, yet that interval is called a major second.

Why are scales so important when dealing with intervals? Can't intervals be measured on their own, separately from a scale? Of course, but most musicians become comfortable with scales and use them to figure out intervals because scales are a point of reference. If you ask a musician what the interval is between A and F, it's likely that he will think first of an A major scale and then determine if F♯ is in the A scale. Since it is, he will lower the F♯ from a major sixth to a minor sixth, and that's the answer.

Notable

When you measure a musical interval, always count the first note as one step. For example, C to G is a fifth because you have to count C as one. This is the most common mistake students make when they are working with musical intervals. They often come up one short because they forget to count the starting spot as one.

QUALITY AND DISTANCE

Intervals have two distinct parts: quality and distance. Quality refers to the first part of an interval, either major or perfect, as you saw from the C major scale intervals. Now, these are not the only intervals in music; these are just the intervals in the C scale. Distance is the simplest part—designations such as second, third, and fourth refer to the absolute distance of the letters. For example, C to E will always be a third apart, because there are three letters from C to E.

The numerical distance is the easiest part of intervals. Determining the quality of an interval is a different story. It's only when you understand all the different qualities that you can name any interval, as you'll see in the following sections.

ENHARMONICS

An interval has to determine the distance from one note to another. As you can see in the C major scale, every interval has a distance and a quality to it. Confusion arises because notes can have more than one name. You might recall enharmonics, where C♯ and D♭ sound the same yet are different notes when written.

In analyzing written music you have to deal with what you are given. When you listen to any interval, you hear the sound—so the distance from C to D♯ will sound just like C to E♭. What you hear is the sound of those notes ringing together, but if you had to analyze it on paper, you'd be looking at two different intervals (one is a minor third and the other is an augmented second) with two different names. The system of intervals has evolved somewhat strangely because enharmonics is built into written music.

Notable

Many modern theorists and composers don't use the traditional intervallic system. Instead, they use a more numerically based system of organization, called set or set theory, which bases intervallic measurements on pure distance-based relationships in half steps. This system solves the ambiguity with enharmonic intervals. So, instead of a major third, it would be a five because a major third is five half steps.

THE SIMPLE INTERVALS

They're Majorly Perfect

There are five distinct types of interval qualities: major, minor, perfect, diminished, and augmented. The distance of an interval always consists of the quality first, followed by the numerical measure of how many notes you are traveling, for example, major sixth. The simple intervals—major, minor, and perfect—are presented here.

MAJOR INTERVALS

Major intervals apply only to distances of seconds, thirds, sixths, and sevenths. A quick trick to spell any major interval is to look at the major scale being used. For example, if you wanted to find out what a major third was from the note E, you could spell the scale, name the third note of the E major scale, and that would be your answer. Many musicians use this method to spell intervals and scales.

The other way to figure out an interval is to look at the distance in half steps (or whole steps). This method precludes knowing the scale. The following table presents all the major intervals and their intervallic distances.

MAJOR INTERVALS

TYPE	DISTANCE IN HALF STEPS	DISTANCE IN WHOLE STEPS
Major second	two	one
Major third	four	two
Major sixth	nine	four and one half
Major seventh	eleven	five and one half

MINOR INTERVALS

Minor intervals are closely related to major intervals, as they also only exist as seconds, thirds, sixths, and sevenths. So, what's the difference between a major and a minor interval? Simply, a minor interval is exactly one half step smaller than a major interval. Look at the next table on minor intervals.

MINOR INTERVALS

TYPE	DISTANCE IN HALF STEPS	DISTANCE IN WHOLE STEPS
Minor second	one	one half
Minor third	three	one and a half
Minor sixth	eight	four
Minor seventh	ten	five

You can name any major interval simply by looking at a major scale and counting. This works for the minor scale, but it's not perfect. If you spell out the minor scale, you do, in fact, get the minor third, minor sixth, and minor seventh, but beware of the second. A minor scale's second note is a major second from the root. If you need to measure a minor second, just remember that a minor second is the smallest interval in music: the half step.

Notable

Strengthen your vocabulary! Instead of talking about half and whole steps, call them by their proper names. A half step is a minor second and a whole step is a major second.

Minor intervals are always exactly one half step lower than their major counterparts. So, if you have to name a minor interval and you're fast at the major intervals, simply lower any major interval exactly one half step and you will be there. The next figure shows how this works.

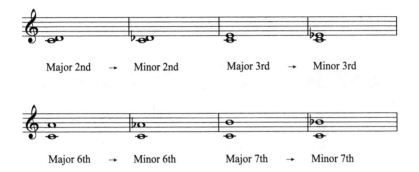

Major Interval → Minor Interval

Major 2nd → Minor 2nd   Major 3rd → Minor 3rd

Major 6th → Minor 6th   Major 7th → Minor 7th

See, that isn't so bad! Just remember that major intervals are the larger of the two intervals when you compare major and minor intervals.

PERFECT INTERVALS

So far, the logic to naming interval quality has made sense: Major intervals come from major scales, and minor intervals (all except one) come from the minor scale. Now you come to perfect intervals, and you may be wondering what is so perfect about them. Here is a brief history lesson. As music was evolving, most music was monophonic, meaning that only one line was sung or played at a time. When musicians became daring enough to add a second line of music, they considered only certain intervals consonant and those were the ones that could be used. In the early days of polyphony, fourths and fifths were commonly used, so perfect seemed to fit because they almost never sounded bad. To modern ears, fourths and fifths don't always sound as nice as thirds or sixths do, but that's just a matter of taste. Back to the intervals! Perfect intervals encompass the following distances: unison (no distance at all), fourth, fifth, and octave.

Notable

The term *octave* includes the prefix *oct*, indicating "eight," so an octave is the distance spanning eight notes. More important, an octave is the same letter name repeated at a higher part of the musical spectrum.

Perfect intervals are fairly easy to spell because all the perfect intervals appear in both the major and the minor scales, so no matter which you are more comfortable spelling in, you'll find all the perfect intervals there. If you're up for counting in steps, look at the next table.

PERFECT INTERVALS

TYPE	DISTANCE IN HALF STEPS	DISTANCE IN WHOLE STEPS
Unison	N/A	N/A
Perfect fourth	five	two and a half
Perfect fifth	seven	three and a half
Perfect octave	twelve	six

In contrast to major intervals that can be made into minor intervals by simply lowering them a half step, the perfect intervals are stuck. If you do anything to a perfect interval (flat or sharp one of the notes), you are changing the interval type away from being perfect. It always becomes something else. What it actually becomes is addressed in the next section.

ADVANCED INTERVALS

Different Can Be Good

There are two more types of intervals that deal with the issue of enharmonic spellings of notes and other anomalies: augmented and diminished intervals.

As you know, the intervals of C to E♭ and C to D♯ sound exactly the same. The only thing that's different is the spelling of the D♯ and the E♭. That's called an enharmonic.

Now, the spelling of those intervals will change as the note changes its name—this is regardless of whether those intervals sound exactly the same. For example, if the interval is spelled C to E♭, the interval is called a minor third. If the interval is spelled C to D♯, you can't call it a minor third anymore. Third intervals are reserved for intervals of three notes (C to E). Since this interval is from C to D, it must be called a second of some sort. In this case, the correct name is an augmented second. Enharmonic spellings give birth to the need for terms such as augmented and diminished intervals.

AUGMENTED INTERVALS

An augmented interval is any interval that is larger than a major or perfect interval. The next figure shows a few examples of augmented intervals.

Augmented Intervals

Augmented 2nd

Augmented 3rd

Augmented 4th

Augmented 5th

Augmented 6th

Traditionally, you can only augment second, third, fourth, fifth, or sixth intervals, and you can only use augmented intervals when the notes are spelled in an unusual way. The logic is "if it's three notes apart, I have to call it some sort of third, and it's larger than a major third." The deciding factor is how the interval is spelled on paper. Use the distance between the notes as your guide. Again, augmented intervals are used when an interval is too large to be called major or perfect.

DIMINISHED INTERVALS

Diminished intervals are more specialized. A diminished interval is an interval that has been made smaller. Typically, diminished intervals are used only to make perfect intervals smaller. In reality, this is just another spelling convention. You can make a fourth or a fifth diminished by lowering any of the perfect intervals one half step. You can also make a minor interval diminished by simply lowering a minor interval one half step. The interval of C to E♭ is a diminished third. The interval of a diminished fifth is commonly called a tritone because, at six half steps, it splits the octave evenly in half (twelve half steps in an octave).

Notable

Both the diminished fifth and the augmented fourth are considered tritones—the spelling is not important, only the distance. The tritone is such a dissonant interval it was called *diabolus in musica* (the devil in music) during the Middle Ages and was something to avoid at all costs.

CHROMATIC INTERVALS

The chromatic scale includes all twelve tones (including all the half tones) in the octave. Thus, chromatic intervals are a semitone apart.

The following figure provides a full chart of every possible interval and enharmonic spelling in one octave to show you how all this lays out. Notice how the number of half steps an interval has is not always the deciding factor in its name. Because of enharmonic spellings, there are pluralities. Always remember to look at the distance between the written notes, and then look for the quality.

Here is another way to understand intervals. If the top note of the interval exists in the major scale of the bottom note, the interval is major or perfect. If not, it's minor, diminished, or augmented. Here is a little chart to help you. Arrows indicate movement of a half step in either direction.

Diminished ⟷ Minor ⟷ Major ⟷ Augmented
Diminished ⟷ Perfect ⟷ Augmented

The following figure shows the chromatic intervals.

All Chromatic Intervals

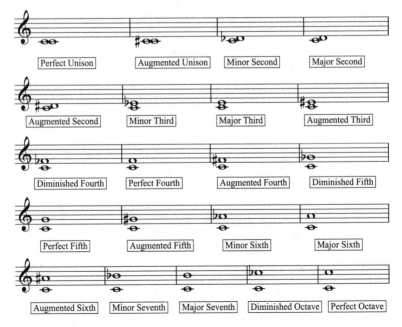

INVERTED AND EXTENDED INTERVALS

Flipping Out

How far is it from C to G? You might say a perfect fifth. You might be right. However, what if the interval went down? What if the C were written higher on the staff than the G? Would it still be a perfect fifth? In this case, it would actually be a perfect fourth.

So far, this text has dealt with ascending intervals. But what happens when you read a descending interval? When you name any interval, such as C to G, you must specify if it's an ascending interval or if it's descending. If the interval ascends, no worries; you've been trained to handle that without a problem. On the other hand, if the interval descends, it's not spelled the same way. A fifth interval, when flipped around, is not a fifth anymore because the musical scale is not symmetrical.

INTERVAL INVERSION

Any interval that ascends can be inverted (flipped upside down). The following figure looks at the example of C to G from the last section. When you flip the perfect fifth, it becomes a perfect fourth. Wouldn't it be great if there were a system to help you invert any interval? Thankfully, there is. You are going to learn to use the rule of nine to invert any interval with ease.

Perfect Fifth   Perfect Fourth

THE RULE OF NINE

The rule of nine is defined as: when any interval is inverted, the sum of the ascending and descending intervals must add up to nine. Using the first example, the interval from C to G is a perfect fifth. The interval from G to C is a perfect fourth. When you add up 5 and 4, you get 9. Test this in a few notation examples in the following figure. What's the inversion of a third? It's a sixth, because 3 and 6 add up to 9. This rule works on any interval.

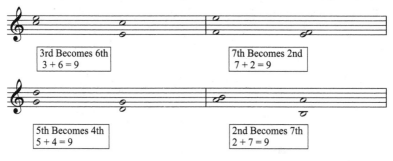

3rd Becomes 6th
3 + 6 = 9

7th Becomes 2nd
7 + 2 = 9

5th Becomes 4th
5 + 4 = 9

2nd Becomes 7th
2 + 7 = 9

INVERTED QUALITIES

When using the rule of nine, it's easy to flip the intervals and get the correct inversion. But the type, or quality, of the interval also changes as you invert it. The rule of nine tells you the name of the interval numerically, but the type of interval that it becomes (major, minor, perfect) will change as the interval is flipped over. This problem has a simple solution. Here is what happens to interval qualities when the intervals invert:

- If the interval was major, it becomes minor when inverted.
- If the interval was minor, it becomes major when inverted.
- If the interval was perfect, it remains perfect when inverted.

Notable

The concept of inverting intervals is actually pretty easy to remember. Major becomes minor, minor becomes major, and perfect stays perfect. As you can see, by using the rule of nine and changing the type of interval accordingly, you can invert intervals like a pro!

HEARING INTERVALS

Name That Tune

Music theory doesn't just have to exist on paper. It can also be measured by ear. We're talking about the amazing human perception known as relative pitch and its elite cousin, absolute or perfect pitch. One way that you can accelerate your music theory ability is to use your ears. While perception is very hard to teach, you can still learn some tricks to make your hearing more acute.

One technique that's used in teaching aural acuity is to relate intervals to famous songs. Can you sing the first few notes of "Here Comes the Bride"? If you said yes, then you can sing a perfect fourth at will. There are several well-known songs that can help you identify musical intervals completely by ear. Since these melodies are largely copyrighted, you won't see examples in written music. If you need to relate these melodies to written music, you can always purchase the sheet music and study from there. Here is a list of common intervals and the songs they relate to:

- **Minor second:** The theme from *Jaws* is an example of an ascending minor second.
- **Major second:** "Happy Birthday" is an example of an ascending major second interval.
- **Minor third:** The first three notes of Beethoven's Fifth Symphony is an example of a descending minor third.
- **Major third:** The first two notes of "When the Saints Go Marching In" is an example of an ascending major third.
- **Perfect fourth:** The first two notes of "Here Comes the Bride" and "Amazing Grace" are examples of ascending perfect fourth intervals.

- **Tritone (diminished fifth/augmented fourth):** The first two notes of "Maria" from *West Side Story* and the theme from *The Simpsons* are examples of ascending tritone intervals.
- **Perfect fifth:** The first four notes of "Twinkle, Twinkle Little Star" is an example of an ascending perfect fifth.
- **Minor sixth:** Minor sixth intervals are hard, as the songs are a bit more obscure. The first two melody notes of the theme to *Doctor Who* is an example of an ascending minor sixth.
- **Major sixth:** The theme music from the NBC chimes is an example of an ascending major sixth interval.
- **Minor seventh:** The first two notes from the theme to Star Trek is an example of an ascending minor seventh.
- **Major seventh:** The first two notes to the chorus of "Take on Me" by a-ha and the first two notes to "Don't Know Why" by Norah Jones are examples of an ascending major seventh.
- **Perfect octave:** The first two notes of "Somewhere over the Rainbow" from *The Wizard of Oz* is an example of an ascending perfect octave.

Notable

What's the difference between relative pitch and perfect pitch? Relative pitch is the ability to discern intervals, qualities, and sounds by ear. You may not know the name of the individual pitches, but you can learn to hear a perfect fourth, or sing it out of thin air. Someone who possesses perfect pitch can identify note names by ear. They can hear single notes or chords/multiple notes at once and identify the names of each of the notes.

Chapter 3

The Major and Minor Scales

A simple formation of notes can bring you into the mind of the composer, allowing you to see what elements are used in composition. The major and minor scales are the first such structural elements that you should study in music. Major scales are multifaceted and are used for melodies and harmonies. Minor scales have their own distinct pattern, construction, order, and, more importantly, their own sound, which is darker and heavier than major scales. Major and minor constitute the two fundamental elements of musical scales used most often in musical theory, writing, and performance.

SCALES DEFINED

Begin at the Beginning and End at the Beginning

A scale is a grouping of notes that makes a key. Most of the scales you will encounter have seven different pitches (but a total of eight notes, including the repeated octave). Some scales contain more than seven notes, and some contain fewer. A scale is defined as a series of eight notes (seven different pitches) that start and end on the same note, which is also called the root. The root names the scale. If a scale starts and ends on C, the root is C and the scale's name is the C something (major, minor, etc.) scale. What that something is depends on its intervallic formula. Aren't you glad you know a thing or two about intervals? Let's take a look at a very basic C major scale in the following figure.

As you can see, the scale starts and ends on C and progresses up every note in order. Since C major contains no sharps and no flats, it's an easy scale to understand and remember. On the piano, it's simply all the white notes. The C scale contains seven different notes: C, D, E, F, G, A, and B. Although the last C isn't counted because it's a repeated note, the major scale has eight notes in total.

What makes this a major scale is not the fact that it uses the notes C-D-E-F-G-A-B-C. That only tells you that it's one particular key. Music theory looks for larger-scale ideas and tries to tie them together. What makes that scale a major scale are the intervals between the notes. If you look at the distance from each note in the scale to the next, you see a pattern of half or whole steps in a series. This series, which you can also call a formula, is exactly what you are going to learn about now.

The next figure shows the C major scale with the intervals defined.

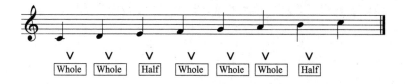

What you come up with is the interval series of Whole, Whole, Half, Whole, Whole, Whole, Half, or WWHWWWH. This is what makes one scale different from any other: the formula of the intervals. As long as that interval formula is present, you have a major scale. It's a perfect system, because you can start on any of the twelve chromatic notes and follow these rules:

1. Pick a root note.
2. Progress up seven notes until you reach the octave.
3. Use the formula of WWHWWWH between your notes to ensure that you have the correct spelling.
4. Make sure that you use any letter only once before the octave.
   If you can follow these rules, you can spell any scale.

HOW SCALES ARE USED IN MUSIC

Scales are really important. As you're going to see, they spin off into all sorts of directions. By itself, a scale is an organization of pitches, which are called sounds. This organization makes scales more than just a set of random pitches; it turns them into a set of sounds that musicians and theorists call a key.

A key is like a family: Everyone's related in some way. When you use a scale to compose a melody, those notes sound as though they belong together. When you stay exclusively in a scale, or a key, you get a very regular and expected sound. Composers use scales to construct melodies. Because keys already have the built-in feeling of belonging together, or better yet, sounding together, it isn't hard to make a scale into a memorable melody. Hundreds of well-known melodies come from a scale of some sort. So think of a scale as a vocabulary for musical phrases, much like letters form words, which in turn form sentences—see the parallels?

Notable

When you play a scale one note at a time, you get a melody. When you take notes from scales and combine them by playing them together, you get harmony. We'll get into these concepts later in this book, but for now, just accept that you can break down the vast majority of music into melody and harmony. Now that you know that scales can give you melodies and harmonies, you can begin to understand how important scales are.

SPELLING SCALES

Now I Know My B, C, Ds

To spell a scale, start out with a root note; in this example it will be A♭, as seen in the following figure.

Next, place the rest of the notes on the staff. Now, don't be too concerned about whether you have the correct intervals or even the right spellings; you just need to have one of each letter name, in order, up to the octave. So simply add B–C–D–E–F–G–A to the next figure.

Now that you have added in the raw notes, you need to add the intervals. The formula is WWHWWWH, so add the intervals between the notes of the scale, as seen here.

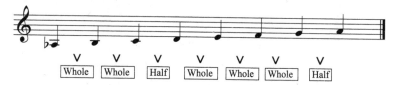

You're nearly done. Now just engage the intervals and make sure your scale is spelled correctly. Follow this process:

- You need a whole step from A♭. A whole step away would be B♭. Add a B♭ to the scale.

- You need a whole step from B♭. A whole step away would be C, which you already have written down, so you don't have to change anything.
- You need a half step from C. A half step away would be D♭, so put a flat in front of the D to make it D♭.
- You need a whole step from D♭. A whole step away is E♭, so make the E an E♭.
- You need a whole step from E♭. A whole step away is F, which you already have, so no change is needed.
- You need a whole step from F. A whole step away is G, which you also already have, so no change is needed.
- You need a half step from G. A half step away is A♭. Change the A to A♭. (Coincidentally, since this is an A♭ scale, every A in this scale is flat, so you could have just made it flat.)

Now, look at the following figure.

That's it! You have an ascending scale that uses every letter of the musical alphabet once. The scale follows the pattern of WWHWWWH, which all major scales follow. Play it on your instrument just to be sure, and that familiar sound will tell you that you're correct.

SOME SCALY THOUGHTS

You have now seen a couple of major scales. This is a good time to pause and point out some very interesting characteristics about scales.

First, scales are unique. They are a bit like DNA and that makes them pretty easy to spot if you know what you're looking for. What does that mean? Well, each scale has a different pitch. No two scales look the same on the surface. Although each scale uses the same interval pattern, that fact is not clear until you analyze the scale. The fact that each scale uses a unique set of pitches is what makes each one unique, and that is something that you can clearly see.

Second, did you notice that the scales that contain sharps use only sharps and never throw in a flat or two? Also, the scales that contain flats use only flats and never sharps? That's right, when you spell scales or analyze music, you will notice that scales have either flats or sharps; you rarely see both sharps and flats in the same scale. These two points will help you understand scales so much better and make your life in music theory so much easier.

Based on which chromatic note the scale starts on, you may get a scale that spells pretty easily. On the other hand, certain scales contain double flats or double sharps in order to keep the WWHWWWH pattern going and use each note in the alphabet. Some spell easily and others are a pain. As a result, some chromatic major scales don't appear often; you typically see scales that spell without constant use of double sharps and double flats.

Due to enharmonic notes, scales can have the same sound but be spelled differently. A good example is A♭ and G♯. The key of A♭ has four flats and isn't too hard to spell or read in. The key of G♯ has six sharps and a double sharp. Which would you rather read in if both scales actually sounded the same? Even though there are twenty-four possible scales, there are only twelve chromatic notes in the scale, and you will find yourself reading in the easiest twelve keys. Remember, music isn't just for the composer; it has to suit the player as well.

Notable

Knowing that flats and sharps are mutually exclusive items in scales should help you spell your scales more accurately. If you're spelling a scale and you see a mixture of flats and sharps, something's wrong. If you see mostly flats and one sharp, something's wrong. Scales will always look cohesive, and that will make your job a bit easier.

SCALE TONES

You Can Call Me by My Name or Number

Each scale has seven tones (eight, if you include the octave). There are two ways to talk about tones: by number and by degree.

SCALE TONES BY NUMBER

In a C major scale, the note C is given the number one because it's the first note of the scale. Then, each of the scale tones, one through seven, can be assigned a different note. This is useful for several reasons. First, the distance of an interval is measured with a number, which is often taken from a scale. Second, since all major scales are made of the same pattern, music theory uses a universal system for naming these scales. If a piece starts on the third note of a scale, you can take that idea and use it in any key. If you simply say, "It starts on E," you lose the context of what scale or key you are in and need extra information in order to work with the idea. Using numbers is a handy way to think about scales and scale tones. A numbering system is also useful in the discussion of chords and chord progressions, since in music theory chord progressions are only labeled with Roman numerals.

SCALE TONES BY DEGREE

You can also describe the tones of the major scale by giving a name, instead of a number, to each degree. This method is traditionally used in classical or academic music-theory contexts, but some of the terms have become universal and you should at least be aware of them. One example is the term *tonic*, which is used to refer to the root (that is, the first chord or tone) of any scale. The following chart gives the names of each note in the major scale.

NAMES OF NOTES IN THE MAJOR SCALE

SCALE DEGREE	NAME
First	Tonic
Second	Supertonic
Third	Mediant
Fourth	Subdominant
Fifth	Dominant
Sixth	Submediant or superdominant
Seventh	Leading tone
Eighth (the octave)	Tonic

These names are also used when talking about chords and chord progressions, so knowing them will aid you in understanding progressions. Although these terms aren't used nearly as much as numbers for the tones, certain names such as tonic, dominant, and leading tone are prevalent in musicians' vernacular. Formal theory, however, uses the names of scale degrees, so now you know what they mean.

Notable

Originating in the thirteenth century, the motet (derived from the French *mot*, meaning "word") is an early example of polyphonic (multivoice) music. Motets were generally liturgical choral compositions written for multiple voices. Johann Sebastian Bach wrote many motets, seven of which still exist today.

THE DEFINITIVE AND DERIVATIVE APPROACHES

Start from Common Elements

Music can convey a mood or feeling based on the key and type of scale. Major scales tend to be bright and upbeat, while minor scales have a darker, moody sound. That doesn't mean the minor scale is of lesser quality; it is merely just another flavor in your musical spice rack. The minor scale is its own entity that has its own formula, intervals, and usage. There are a few ways to look at the minor scale: one is the definitive approach and the other is the derivative approach.

THE DEFINITIVE APPROACH

In the previous explanation of intervals, the example of the C minor scale illustrated some minor intervals and also showed a contrast against C major. The next figure shows the C minor scale.

At this point you know that C major has no sharps or flats, and that's what makes it such an easy key to work with. Now, if you look at the previous figure again, you'll notice that it's different. Sure, it's a different scale, even though it has the same root, C. You learned about the differences in the intervals in this scale in Chapter 2, but now you need to learn the underpinnings of the intervals between the notes so you can understand a formula that enables you to spell any minor scale. Remember that theory is an attempt to find universal parts of music—that is, elements that apply over the entire range of music. Simply knowing that a C minor scale is spelled C–D–E♭–F–G–A♭–B♭ allows you to recognize, spell, and work with only one key. However, if you look at the scale for its intervallic content, you can take that information and apply it anywhere. It's time to break the scale into pieces. The next figure shows the pattern of half and whole steps that are present in the C minor scale.

Not surprisingly, there is a different interval pattern here than in the major scale. It is WHWWHWW. You can use that interval pattern as a construction blueprint and spell any scale you want. Now take a step-by-step look at how to create any minor scale.

First, start out with a root note, such as C, as seen in the next figure.

Now place the rest of the notes on the staff. Don't be concerned with whether you have the correct intervals or even the right spellings. You just need to have one of each letter name, in order, up to the octave. So simply add a D–E–F–G–A–B to this next figure.

You have the raw notes in; next you need to add the intervals. The formula is WHWWHWW, so add the intervals between the notes of the scale, as seen here.

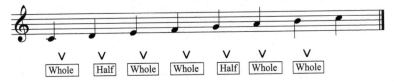

You're nearly done. All you have to do is engage the intervals and make sure your scale is spelled correctly. Here's the process:

- You need a whole step from C. A whole step away would be D, which you already have.
- You need a half step from D. A half step away would be E♭, so add a flat before the E.
- You need a whole step from E♭. A whole step away would be F, which you already have.
- You need a whole step from F. A whole step away is G, which you also already have.
- You need a half step from G. A half step away is A♭, so add a flat before the A.
- You need a whole step from A♭. A whole step away is B♭, so place a flat before B.
- You need a whole step from B♭. A whole step away is C.

Now to see your full scale, look at the following figure.

That's it! You now have an ascending scale that uses every letter of the musical alphabet once. Your scale follows the pattern of WHW-WHWW, which all minor scales follow.

THE DERIVATIVE APPROACH

Being able to form scales from pure intervals is a common and useful way to spell scales. Another convenient way is to derive them from major scales. Many students become comfortable with spelling major scales and find it easy to recall them. If you look at the difference between a major scale and a minor scale with the same root, you can form another way to spell minor scales: deriving them from modifications to the major scales. The next figure shows a C major scale on the top line and a C minor scale on the bottom line.

The Highlighted Notes Are The Only Changes Between C Major and C Minor

The scales are very similar. The notes C, D, F, and G stay the same. Only the third, sixth, and seventh notes are changing from the major scale to the minor scale. More specifically, the third, sixth, and seventh scale degrees are lowered exactly one half step from their spelling in the major scale to make the minor scale.

Notable

It is important to be comfortable with all the different ways to spell scales because you never know which one will work the best for you!

Since you have dealt with intervals in detail, take a closer look at what happened when you went from the major scale to the minor scale. Simply, the intervals of the major third, major sixth, and major seventh (when measured from the root of C) are all changed from major intervals to minor intervals simply by lowering each of the intervals one half step. Remember from the discussion of intervals, the only difference between a major interval and a minor interval is that the minor interval is one half step smaller than the major interval, or vice versa.

This means that any major scale can become a minor scale by lowering the third, sixth, and seventh scale degrees one half step. This method derives the minor scale from the spelling of the major scale—using the derivative approach.

DEGREES IN MINOR SCALES

Know Your Position

Just like major scales, minor scales can also have scale degrees. As with major scales, you can refer to the tones in the minor scale numerically, just as you did when looking at the derivative approach for spelling minor scales (talking about the third, sixth, and seventh scale degrees). As a refresher, here is an explanation of scale degrees.

The other way to describe the tones of the minor scale is to give a distinct name to each degree. This method is traditionally used in classical and academic music-theory contexts, but some of the terms have become universal, and you should at least be aware of them. The term *tonic*, used to refer to the root of any scale, is an example of the names given to each note in the minor scale. The following table shows how to name each note in the minor scale.

NAMES OF NOTES IN THE MINOR SCALE

SCALE DEGREE	NAME
First	Tonic
Second	Supertonic
Third	Mediant
Fourth	Subdominant
Fifth	Dominant
Sixth	Submediant or superdominant
Seventh	Leading tone
Eighth (the octave)	Tonic

These names are also used when discussing chords and chord progressions, so knowing them will aid you in understanding progressions. Although these terms aren't used nearly as much as numbers, musicians commonly refer to certain names such as tonic, dominant, and leading tone. Formal theory uses the names of scale degrees, so now you'll know what they mean.

MULTIPLE SCALES—SCALE CLARITY

In contrast to the major scale, which comes in only one variety, the minor scale comes in a few different forms. What you have begun to explore is the natural minor scale. When people talk about minor scales, they are typically talking about the natural minor scale, which has the formula of WHWWHWW. However, there are two other minor scales that have different interval patterns than the natural minor scale: harmonic and melodic minor.

Notable

The natural minor scale is a naturally occurring extension of the major scale, also called a related or relative minor. Relative minors are discussed later in this book. The other minor scales (harmonic and melodic minor) are derivatives of the natural minor scales.

Harmonic and melodic minor scales are slightly controversial in traditional music theory. Some theorists argue that they are not true scales because they are not naturally occurring patterns. But music theory is about identifying what is seen and heard in music, and whether you believe that scales should have their own names, these minor scales are found in music often enough that it is important to know about them. In any case, harmonic and melodic minor scales are part of the basic level of theory knowledge.

HARMONIC MINOR

The harmonic minor is the first variation of the minor scale you should know. It's a simple change of the natural minor scale, formed by raising the seventh note one half step. Doing so creates a leading tone to the scale. It simply gives a very strong pull from the last note of the scale back to the tonic. All major scales have a built-in leading tone, but natural minor scales do not; they have a whole step between the sixth and seventh tones. Interestingly, this is not why composers use the harmonic minor scale. The name of the scale gives some insight into why the scale exists. The raising of the seventh tone gives composers a slightly better harmonic palette to work with; it gives better chords. The harmonic minor scale provides a major chord on the dominant degree and a diminished chord on the leading-tone degree. Both of these chords are extremely important to composers and musicians and are used so frequently that the harmonic minor scale actually became a scale.

The D harmonic minor scale is shown in the following figure.

The formula of the scale is interesting as it is no longer strictly kept to whole and half steps. In fact, between the sixth and seventh tone, there is a step and a half (an augmented second to be more exact). That large leap is awkward melodically.

Melodically, the harmonic minor scale is awkward to work with. So composers created the melodic minor scale to solve this dilemma.

MELODIC MINOR

The melodic minor scale is created by raising the sixth and seventh tones of a natural minor scale one half step each. The whole point is to smooth out the skip between the sixth and the seventh tones in the harmonic minor scale. The raised seventh tone in harmonic minor is crucial to minor scale harmony, but the scale played alone sounds strange. By raising the sixth as well, the melodic minor scale works better for melodies and harmonies. The augmented second interval between the sixth and seventh tone disappears, and it's back to whole and half steps.

Because the change in the scale makes it melodically smoother, it's called the melodic minor scale. Both the harmonic and melodic minor scales fall under the umbrella of basic music theory, which is important to understand in order to read music. The next figure presents the melodic minor scale in the key of D minor.

Chapter 4

Musical Keys and Key Signatures

As you learned earlier, intervals are the smallest element of music. Intervals combine to form scales. Scales, in turn, make up melody and harmony, the lifeblood of music. The key is the next major level of organization and one of the major elements of musical analysis. In this chapter, you will learn what makes a key, how to identify a key, and why you should care about the musical key.

THE MUSICAL KEY

The DNA of Music

Now that you have explored the primary scales that make up music, it's time to explore the key. The key is the first level of organization in tonal music—that is, music that is composed of keys, chords, and scales. Of course, there are forms of music that do not rely on keys, such as modern and atonal music. For the purpose of this book, tonal music makes up the majority of music from the common-practice period (circa 1685–1900) and is still very much in use today. The study of theory starts in the common-practice period and moves forward. If you want to study tonal music, keys are going to be very important.

The concept of musical keys is closely tied to scales, both major and minor. A key defines the basic pitches for a piece of music. It does not have to use those notes exclusively, but the majority of the notes will come from the scale of that key. You know from studying the major and minor scales that no two scales are ever spelled alike. Because each scale/key is unique, it is fairly easy to spot them in music and understand some of the musical structure involved. You can think of keys as the DNA of music.

Notable

Key signatures correspond to major and minor scales. Since a great deal of written music adheres to major and minor scales, key signatures are a convenient way to indicate the keys and scales that are frequently used. Key signatures are also a visual method of determining the key of a piece of music.

A key is a slightly abstract concept, which can be a challenge to describe. A key defines what notes can be used to create an expected sound, such as consonant and not dissonant. As you progress as a musician, keys and key signatures will become more important than just defining what notes to play. Keys can give you a glimpse into the mind of the composer and help you unravel how music is composed. In any event, you need to know a lot about keys and their key signatures if you want to be a competent music theorist.

WHAT IS A KEY SIGNATURE?

You know all about sharps and flats and can comfortably spell scales in any key. That knowledge is one step removed from real music and how it functions. Observe the spelling of the A major scale in the first figure versus the same scale with a key signature shown in the second figure. Instead of spelling each sharp and flat, you can use a key signature to make all the Fs, Cs, and Gs sharp. Most musicians would rather read the second figure any day of the week.

In other words, a key signature is used to indicate that a certain note or notes are going to be sharp or flat for the entire piece. It cleans up the written music for the reader and eliminates the need for the sharp and flat symbols that would otherwise appear throughout. A good reader is used to reading in key signatures and prefers them.

THE KEY SIGNATURES

Key signatures apply to the common keys/scales and rarely deal with the enharmonic keys. Students often encounter the circle of keys, a graphic representation of the typical keys. Since every key or scale has its unique spelling, each of the keys looks different as well. Each single key signature corresponds to one single major key. Here is the circle of keys.

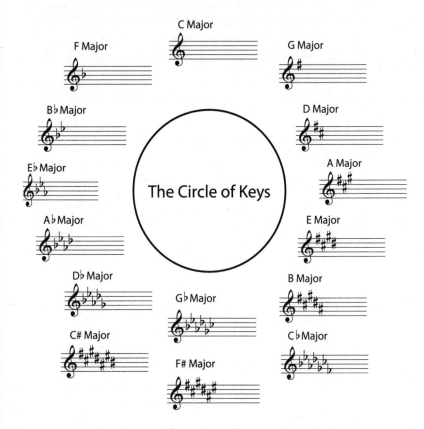

KEYS CHANGE

Music does not need to stay in one key; key changes happen frequently in music. The way to change keys and identify key changes will become much clearer when you understand harmony. For now, look at the circle of keys and make a few assumptions that will be explained as the book progresses.

Here are the rules:

- When music changes keys, it changes to a closely related key.
- The closest related key is the relative minor.
- The other close keys that you can modulate to are next to the original key on the key circle (either one key to the left or one key to the right).
- The other modulation you can make is from a major to a parallel minor; for example, C major to C minor.

ALL ABOUT KEY SIGNATURES

Name That Key

Key signatures use a specific system. Not just any note can appear in a key signature. There is an order and a logic that makes key signatures understandable. There are two varieties: sharp key signatures and flat key signatures (excluding C major, which has no sharps or flats). A key signature displays only sharps or only flats, never both. Within these groupings of sharps or flats there is an order to how individual notes appear.

Do you remember reading that proper scale spellings also result in either sharps or flats? Scales and key signatures show you the same information, which is exactly why they help you understand more about the music.

Sharps appear in key signatures in a specific order: F♯, C♯, G♯, D♯, A♯, E♯, and B♯.

They always follow that order. If a key has one sharp, it will be an F♯. If a key has two sharps, it will have F♯ and C♯. It always works through the pattern in the same way. A great way to remember the order of sharps is to use a little mnemonic device: Father Charles Goes Down And Ends Battle. The first letter of each word corresponds to the sharps as they appear.

Notable

Even though key signatures may appear confusing at first, most musicians would have a hard time reading without them. Constant flats and sharps placed throughout music are more challenging to read than a single key signature.

Just like sharps, flats appear in a specific order every time. Here is the order: B♭, E♭, A♭, D♭, G♭, C♭, and F♭.

There is also an easy way to remember the order of flats: Just reverse the mnemonic for sharps! <u>B</u>attle <u>E</u>nds <u>A</u>nd <u>D</u>own <u>G</u>oes <u>C</u>harles's <u>F</u>ather. One saying gets you both sharps and flats—pretty convenient!

If you stare at the circle of keys long enough, you might memorize what each key represents. However, there are a few tricks that can help you. On the flat side, the first key is F, which starts with the same letter as the word *flat*. After that, BEAD contains the names of the next four flat keys. That's a handy way to learn some of the keys. The sharp side is a bit harder. BEAD appears again on the right side. However, there are two little tricks you can learn for instantly naming a key just by looking at it.

THE SHARP KEY TRICK

For any key that has a sharp in it, naming the key is as simple as following two easy steps. First, find the last sharp (the one all the way to the right). Once you've found and named the note that corresponds to the same line or space the sharp is on, go one note higher, and you've named the key. Look at the next figure. The last sharp in this key is A♯. Going one note above this is the note B. Five sharps is, indeed, the correct key signature for the key of B major. You can check the trusty circle just to make sure.

The good news is that this trick works on every key that has a sharp in it. To find the name of a sharp key:

1. Name the last sharp, the one all the way to the right.
2. Go one note higher than the last sharp, and that's the name.

Unfortunately, it works only when you're looking at a key. For everything else, refer to the circle of keys and the order of sharps and flats.

THE FLAT KEY TRICK

The flat keys have a different naming trick. When you see a piece of music that has flats, find the second-to-last flat. The name of that flat is the name of your key. Look at the following figure. This key has two flats and the second-to-last flat is B♭. The name of the key with two flats is B♭. This is an easy trick.

There is one exception: the key with one flat, F major. Since this key has only one flat, there is no second-to-last flat. In this case, you'll just have to memorize that F has one flat (which is B♭).

To find the name of a flat key:

1. Find the second-to-last flat (from the right).
2. The name of the flat note you find is the name of the key.

Just remember the exception—the key of F major has one flat and therefore the rule does not work for it. For the other keys, it works like a charm!

THE CIRCLE MOVES IN FOURTHS AND FIFTHS

The circle of keys is often referred to as the circle of fifths or the circle of fourths. The keys are arranged in the circle in a fairly logical way. The key of C, with no sharps or flats, sits squarely in the center, and the sharp keys move around the right side, each key increasing the number of sharps by one. The flat keys move to the left, increasing their flats by one as they progress.

If you move to the right from C, each key is a perfect fifth apart. In addition, the order of sharps as they appear in the key signatures is also in perfect fifths starting from F♯.

If you move to the left from C, each key is exactly a perfect fourth apart. Conveniently, the flats as they appear in the key signature are also a perfect fourth apart, starting from B♭.

Think about these two points:

1. Sharp keys move in fifths around the circle, and the sharps are fifths apart.
2. Flat keys move in fourths around the circle, and the flats are fourths apart.

When you move in one direction in the key circle, you move in fifths; when you move in the opposite direction, you move in fourths. Remember the explanation about interval inversion: A perfect fifth becomes a perfect fourth when inverted. A fifth up is the same as a fourth down. The same explanation applies to the order of sharps and flats. The sharps are spaced a fifth apart starting from F, and the flats are spaced a fourth apart starting from B. Interestingly, when you spell out all the sharps and read them backward (backward = inverted = in fourths), you get the order of flats.

RELATIVE MINOR KEYS

It's a Major Deal

Up to this point, you have learned solely about major key signatures and their related major scales; the circle of keys and the tricks for naming the keys all refer to major keys.

Of course, you know about minor scales, and where there are scales, there are keys. The good news is that all the minor scales and keys share the same key signatures, which you already know. The bad news is that they aren't the same as the major keys. Never fear, there are some easy ways to learn the minor keys as well.

SHARED SIGNATURES

Every major key and its corresponding key signature serve a dual function. They indicate a major key, and they indicate a minor key as well. The concept is called relative keys and related minor. Simply put, every major scale/key has a minor scale/key hiding inside it. For now, you'll learn how to figure out the name of the minor keys. The next figure shows the key signature for E♭ major. The same key signature can signify the key of C minor.

Is This E♭ or C Minor?

How is this possible? Well, simply put, if you spell the E♭ major scale and the C minor scale, you will see that they share the same key signature. The other thing that you are seeing is a mode: The minor scale is a mode of the major scale. Modes are discussed later, but for now just accept that since they share the same pitches, even if they are in a different order, they are related.

Notable

Looking at a key signature alone won't tell you whether your piece is in the major or the minor key. You need to investigate the piece of music itself.

NAMING MINOR KEYS

To name a minor key signature, first name the major key. Then count up six notes (up a major sixth) or down three (down a minor third). Either way, you arrive at the same note. In the case of C major, counting up six notes brings you to A. C major and A minor share the same key signature and are referred to as related keys. When you look at a piece without sharps or flats in the signature, it could just as easily be in A minor as C major. You won't know for sure by just looking at a key signature because music isn't that easy. You have to look at the harmony and that comes later in this book. For now, concentrate on being able to name minor keys from major key signatures.

When naming a minor key, be careful to look at the key signature when you are doing so. Simply counting up six notes or down three notes may not give you the correct key. If the note you pick has a sharp or a flat in that key, the name of the minor key needs to reflect that. You're not just counting up six letters; you have to mind the key signature. It's much easier to use the interval of a major sixth, which has a clear name. Look at the next figure. In this case, the sixth note is not just C, but C♯, so the name of the key has to reflect that. The key of E major has a relative minor of C♯ minor.

The 6th note names the relative minor.

The following figure shows the full circle of keys with both the major and the minor keys.

DETERMINING THE KEY

The Circle of Keys
With Relative Minor Keys

You can determine the key by looking at the signature and checking your circle of keys. This action will give you at least two answers: the major and the relative minor key. In a way, this is your first step toward musical analysis, but it is more than just looking at a key signature. The answer is rarely that simple. Or is it?

One old trick suggests that you can look at the first and last notes of any piece to determine the key. Now, although this rarely works because music involves so many variables, sometimes it does work. If you look at a key signature and your choices are either a minor or a major key (C major or A minor, for example), you could scan the piece for Cs or As and that may answer your question. Then again, it may not. While it is true that many pieces conclude on the tonic note of the key, that fact only tells you where the piece ended, not where it went in the middle.

If you are trying to decipher what key you're in, the first and last note (or chord) may give you a basic answer. The answer that works in every piece can only be found by looking at the details of the piece—and that involves the key signature, the harmony, and the per-note changes that exist throughout the piece. Since you know about scales in detail now, you can work on one more aspect of keys based on minor scales and their typical visual patterns.

MINOR KEYS ON PAPER

It's Not an Accident

In a great deal of music, you rarely see the natural minor scale; instead you see the harmonic or melodic minor scales. When you are looking at a piece of music and the key signature gives you two possible answers, look inside the music itself for more clues.

Notable

Both the harmonic minor scale and the melodic minor scale have alterations via accidentals. For a minor scale to function in the traditional sense, it needs this alteration. More specifically, the leading tone needs to be raised, which will cause a subsequent sharp, flat, or natural where it doesn't normally belong.

If the piece is in the major key, it won't need any additional accidentals (sharps or flats) to function. That's not to say that pieces in major keys never have accidentals, but minor keys have very specific accidentals. If you know what to look for, you should have no problem finding out the answer.

A leading tone is the seventh note of a scale. In the case of the harmonic and melodic minor scale, it's raised one half step higher than in the natural minor scale. For example, in A minor, the leading tone in the natural scale is G; if you raise it, it becomes a G♯. Now, remember that A minor and C major share a key signature that has no sharps or flats. So, you're looking at a piece with no key signature and scattered throughout the piece are a bunch of G♯s. The final note of the piece is A. Chances are that you are in A minor, or at least you were in A minor for a part of that piece and concluded there. By the same token, if you see a piece with no key signature and nothing but G♮s, you're in C major, because the G♯ is the leading tone of A minor.

Look at the next figure. What key do you think it is?

At first glance, the key signature has one sharp, so it could be G major or E minor. The first thing to do is look for accidentals. Do you have any? Yes, there is a D♯ throughout the piece. The next step is to determine if that is just an accidental or if it is a minor-scale leading tone. In the key of E minor, the leading tone is a raised seventh note, which happens to be D♯. The fact that the piece starts and ends on E drives home the point that you are in the key of E minor.

See, that wasn't so hard. It shows you that you cannot judge the key based on the signature alone—you must look at the material within the piece to be absolutely sure. Knowing what the leading tones are will make it much easier to understand the differences between key signatures and their relative minor scales.

Notable

To find the leading tones for minor keys, just find the seventh note of the scale. Instead of going up seven notes, go down one note. Then make sure it's a half step away. For example, the leading tone for C minor is B♮ because B and C are a half step apart. In D minor, the leading tone is C♯.

Chapter 5

Modes and Other Scales

It is true that major and minor scales make up the majority of the scales that you encounter in everyday life. However, both traditional and modern music theory include other scales as well. Mode is a term that music students hear often and rarely understand. In addition, you'll hear about pentatonic, diminished, and whole-tone scales.

MODES

The Other Side of Scales

The first place to deepen your understanding of scales is right back at the major scale. Many classical musicians don't deal with modes early on in their study, but jazz and rock players do. There are several reasons for this musical divide, which will become clear as you learn more about modes.

DEFINING MODES

The simplest definition of a mode is that it is a displaced major scale. First, what does the term *displaced* mean? Take the F major scale: F–G–A–B♭–C–D–E–F. As you know, what makes it an F major scale is that the note F (the tonic degree) has the most weight; the scale wants to stop on the high F when you play it.

Now, what if you were to use the same vocabulary—that is, use the same F–G–A–B♭–C–D–E–F pitches (the F major scale)—but make a different note the root? What if the scale looked like this: D–E–F–G–A–B♭–C–D? If the D sounded like the root note (which is based on the context of the piece), then you have an official mode. You have a bit more than a mode, actually.

If you reread the last paragraph, you'll notice that an F scale is spelled from D. Is there a special relationship between F and D? Well, they are a sixth apart. Hmm, sixth note of a major scale, where have you heard that before? Try looking in the previous chapter in the section "Naming Minor Keys." Remember the trick you learned there, to find the relative minor by going up six notes. Using this example, you can spell an F major scale starting from D, its sixth note, and it's called a mode. It's the D minor scale and a mode of F major.

So, you see that minor scales are also modes. The notes D–E–F–G–A–B♭–C–D form a D minor scale. A mode is formed when you call any other note besides the original root of the scale the root. The minor scale is just one example of a mode, one that you already know. But wait, there's more. Because a major scale has seven notes, there are seven modes.

Notable

In a classical music-theory class, modes are commonly referred to as church modes because of their widespread use in sacred music—especially Gregorian chant. Relegating modes to historical learning is a disservice, however. Modes are alive and well in modern music, especially jazz.

MODAL HISTORY

Modes gained prominence during the golden age of the Gregorian chant, circa A.D. 900, when they were used to compose the melodies of vocal plainchant. Modes stayed in use throughout the medieval era with some modification. The baroque and prebaroque periods used major and minor scales exclusively instead of modes. For all intents and purposes, modes lay dormant throughout the baroque era, the classical era, and most (but not all) of the romantic era.

Even though impressionist composers revived modes, it wasn't until jazz musicians started using them in improvisation and composition that modes became a useful part of music curricula. Today, all music students learn about modes, but rock and jazz players tend to utilize them more frequently.

MODAL SCALES

Shift Your Thinking

Each and every major scale can be looked at from seven different angles—one mode starting from each note in the scale. While modes theoretically come from parent major scales, it's easiest to think of them as their own entities.

IONIAN

Ionian is the first mode to learn about, and you already know it. The Ionian scale is simply the major scale. It follows the interval pattern WWHWWWH. The following figure shows an F Ionian mode. Since the Ionian mode is simply the traditional major scale, think of Ionian as the proper name for a major scale.

DORIAN

The Dorian mode, the first of the displaced scales, is a major scale played from its second note. If you continue to use F major as the parent scale, the Dorian mode in this key starts from the note G and progresses up the same notes. The next figure shows the G Dorian scale. The G Dorian scale uses the interval pattern WHWWWHW.

There is a very important aspect to understand about modes. The G Dorian scale comes from the F major scale and shares all the same notes. This is an important learning tool, but all musicians need to learn the modes as "their own thing." The Dorian mode is a scale unto itself, with its own distinct sound. If you look at the notes of G Dorian (G–A–B♭–C–D–E–F–G), you might notice that the G Dorian scale looks a lot like the traditional G minor scale (G–A–B♭–C–D–E♭–F–G)—and you're right. The only difference is that the G Dorian scale contains an E♮ and the G minor scale contains an E♭.

You could look at the Dorian scale as a minor-type scale, with an altered sixth note. In this case, the sixth note is raised up a half step. It's very much like a flavored minor scale. Today modes are used to spice up traditional major and minor scales that may sound overused and dated. As you'll see, all the rest of the modes closely resemble either a traditional major or a traditional minor scale.

Notable

When you think of the parent-scale relationship between each mode, don't fall into the trap of thinking that each mode has to be related to its parent scale. Using the minor scale as an example again, you don't have to think about its related major scale, do you? No, it can stand on its own. The same holds true for all the modes. Learn to see them on their own if you plan to use them quickly.

PHRYGIAN

Phrygian, the third mode, is the result of forming a scale starting from the third note of the parent major scale. Using F major as the parent scale, the Phrygian scale is an A Phrygian scale. It uses the interval pattern HWWWHWW (see the following figure). Phrygian has a distinct sound and is often used by Spanish composers.

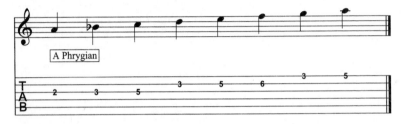

The A Phrygian scale (A–Bb–C–D–E–F–G–A) looks very much like a traditional A minor scale (A–B–C–D–E–F–G–A). The only difference is that the A Phrygian scale lowers the second note a half step. You could say that Phrygian is just a minor scale with a lowered second note—and you'd be right.

LYDIAN

The fourth mode of the major scale is the Lydian mode. Using F as a parent scale, you come to the Bb Lydian scale. Lydian uses the interval pattern WWWHWWH. See the following.

The Lydian mode provides a striking, beautiful, and bright sound. It's used by film composers to convey uplifting spirit and is a favorite of jazz and rock composers. The Lydian scale is so bright and happy that it's no surprise it's closely related to the major scale. The B♭ Lydian scale is spelled B♭–C–D–E–F–G–A–B♭, which resembles a traditional B♭ major scale (B♭–C–D–E♭–F–G–A–B♭). The only difference between B♭ Lydian and B♭ major is that a Lydian scale raises the fourth note of the major scale a half step. So, B♭ Lydian is a B♭ major scale with a raised fourth note. The raised fourth tone results in a bright and unusual sound and allows the plain major scale to have a unique overall effect.

MIXOLYDIAN

The fifth mode of the major scale is called the Mixolydian mode. Using the parent scale of F, our fifth mode is C Mixolydian. C Mixolydian, or Mixo as it's commonly abbreviated, uses the interval pattern of WWH-WWHW. See the following figure.

C Mixolydian

The Mixolydian mode is closely related to the major scale but is slightly darker sounding. The C Mixolydian scale (C–D–E–F–G–A–B♭–C) closely resembles the C major scale (C–D–E–F–G–A–B–C). The only difference is that the Mixolydian scale lowers the seventh note of the major scale a half step. The lowered seventh note gives the Mixolydian mode a bluesy, dark color, leading away from the overly peppy major scale. Because of this, it's a staple of blues, rock, and jazz players who want to darken the sound of major scales. It also coincides with one of the principal chords of jazz, blues, and rock music: the dominant seventh chord (C7, which you're going to learn all about later in the book).

AEOLIAN

The sixth mode of the major scale is the Aeolian mode. Previously you learned that minor scales are derived from the sixth note of a major scale. That's right, the Aeolian mode is the natural minor scale. This is another mode that you already know. Aeolian is the proper name for natural minor. Using the parent key of F major, our sixth mode brings us to D Aeolian. You'll also remember that the keys of F major and D minor are related keys—F Ionian and D Aeolian are related modes from the same parent scale. The D Aeolian scale uses the interval formula WHWWHWW. See the next figure.

Since the Aeolian scale is an exact minor scale, there's no need to compare it to another major or minor scale. Some players are still more comfortable with major scales. If this applies to you, just look at Aeolian as a major scale with lowered third, sixth, and seventh notes.

LOCRIAN

The seventh and final mode is called the Locrian mode. In our parent scale of F major, the seventh mode is E Locrian. E Locrian mode uses the interval pattern HWWHWWW. See the following figure.

The E Locrian scale (E–F–G–A–B♭–C–D–E) looks a lot like an E minor scale (E–F♯–G–A–B–C–D–E). The only difference is that the Locrian scale has a lowered second and a lowered fifth note. The Locrian mode has a very distinct sound that you won't encounter often. Nevertheless, it completes your knowledge of modes, so it's good to know it.

MODES ON THEIR OWN

You now know modes in relation to a parent scale. If someone were to ask you to spell a C♯ Lydian scale, however, it might be quite an ordeal. First, you have to remember which number mode it is, then you have to backtrack and find the parent scale, and then you can spell the scale correctly. It's much easier to understand modes than to have to take several steps to puzzle them out.

Here is a recap of the modes, their interval formulas, and easy ways to relate the scales:

MODES, SCALES, AND INTERVAL FORMULAS

MODE	SCALE	INTERVAL FORMULA	
Mode 1	Ionian	WWHWWWH	Ionian is the major scale
Mode 2	Dorian	WHWWWHW	Dorian is a minor scale with a raised sixth note
Mode 3	Phrygian	HWWWHWW	Phrygian is a minor scale with a lowered second note
Mode 4	Lydian	WWWHWWH	Lydian is a major scale with a raised fourth note
Mode 5	Mixolydian	WWHWWHW	Mixolydian is a major scale with a lowered seventh note
Mode 6	Aeolian	WHWWHWW	Aeolian is the minor scale
Mode 7	Locrian	HWWHWWW	Locrian is a minor scale with lowered second and fifth notes

OTHER IMPORTANT SCALES

Last but Not Least

Major scales, minor scales, and modes make up the majority of the scales encountered in Western music. However, they are not the only important scales; scales come in many different shapes and sizes, especially as you move throughout history.

MAJOR PENTATONIC

Pentatonic scales contain only five notes per octave as opposed to major and minor scales, which contain seven. The name *pentatonic* reflects this distinction, as the prefix *penta* is Greek for "five," and *tonic* means "tones" or "notes." The pentatonic scales are widely used in folk, liturgical, rock, and jazz music. Pentatonic scales come in two varieties: major and minor.

Notable

The major pentatonic is a mainstay of folk, blues, rock, and country music. Famous melodies such as "Mary Had a Little Lamb" and "London Bridge" were composed using only the major pentatonic scale. If you like to improvise solos, the major pentatonic is a basic and essential scale for improvisation over major tonalities found in music genres such as rock, jazz, and blues.

The major pentatonic is a five-note scale derived from the major scale. It simply omits two notes—the fourth and seventh tones—from the major scale. In the key of G, the major pentatonic scale is G–A–B–D–E. Stated another way, the G major pentatonic is the first, second, third, fifth, and sixth notes of a major scale. See the following figure.

G Major Pentatonic

MINOR PENTATONIC

The minor pentatonic scale is also derived from a scale with two notes omitted (just not the same ones as the major pentatonic). A minor pentatonic scale leaves out the second and sixth tones from a natural (or more formally, Aeolian) minor scale. In the key of D, a minor pentatonic scale is D–F–G–A–C. You could also say that the scale is the first, third, fourth, fifth, and seventh notes of a natural minor scale. See the next figure.

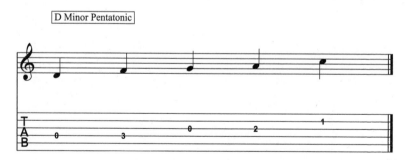

D Minor Pentatonic

WHOLE TONE

The whole-tone scale is built entirely with whole steps. Because it uses the same intervals, the whole-tone scale is considered a symmetric scale. Using whole steps from C, a C whole-tone scale is C–D–E–F♯–G♯–A♯. Note that the whole-tone scale is a six-note scale (see the next figure)—not five notes like our pentatonic scales, or seven notes like major and minor scales, but six.

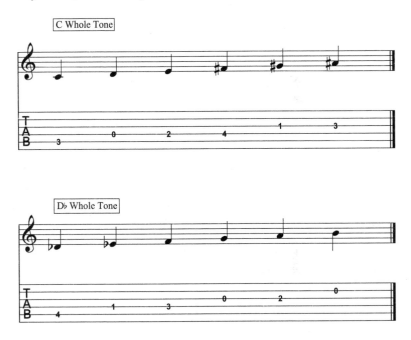

There are only two different whole-tone scales. Forming whole-tone scales from anywhere other than C or D♭ will yield the same notes as the C or D♭ whole-tone scales. See for yourself in the next figure.

Notice how both the C and D whole-tone scales contain the same notes. This makes them very easy to learn and play. You see whole-tone scales in romantic music and jazz music.

Notable

Jazz pianist Thelonious Monk loved the whole-tone scale and used it in many of his recorded improvised jazz solos. The whole-tone scale was his trademark. He wasn't the first to use it, but boy, did he like it!

DIMINISHED/OCTATONIC SCALES

The last scale is also symmetric and is built using repeating intervals. The diminished scale is based on repeating intervals, always half steps and whole steps. There are two varieties of diminished scales: one that starts with the pattern of whole-step, half-step intervals, and one that uses a half-step, whole-step interval pattern. The following figure shows the two varieties of diminished scales, both starting from C. A diminished scale is also called octatonic, meaning it is an eight-note scale. This is the first scale that exceeds seven individual notes.

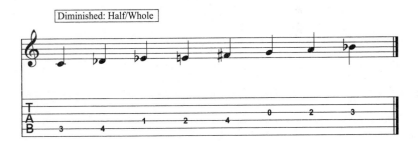

Chapter 6

Chords

The next step in your musical journey is to look at chords and the basic foundations of harmony. Intervals combine into chords, and harmonies emerge from those chords, providing the foundation of tonality, which is the language spoken by the music you hear. To broaden your knowledge of chords you'll also learn about seventh chords. Seventh chords are used extensively throughout music, and they are the next logical step after you understand triads.

CHORDS

Think Three

Essentially, a chord is three or more notes sounded simultaneously. The simplest kind of chord is a triad, which begins with the prefix *tri*, meaning "three." A triad is a three-note chord, and the intervals between the notes (as you will learn soon) are always thirds apart—yet another use of the prefix *tri*.

Just like intervals, chords come in different qualities. The quality refers to the type of chord it is, which is always based on some sort of construction rule. The basic chord qualities for triads are major, minor, augmented, and diminished. Those are the same qualities that the intervals had (excluding perfect). So to recap, a chord, at its simplest, is a three-note triad with intervals that are thirds apart and notes that ring together. Before you go any further, look at the next figure to see a simple C major triad.

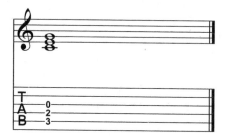

This is the simplest way to look at a chord, essentially the model or prototype voicing, but rarely do you see chords in such clear order. You should think of triads as model chords. They are the simplest way to spell a chord. Unfortunately, rarely do you ever see such models of perfection in music. What you do see are chord voicings. A voicing is a rearrangement of the notes of the triad without adding or taking away from the essential ingredients (in the case of C major: C–E–G).

The next figure shows what a guitarist plays when asked to play a C major chord.

If you compare this chord with the pure triad in the previous figure, you can see that while they appear visually different on the page, in fact, they contain the same elements. Both chords contain the principal notes C, E, and G, but the guitar voicing repeats the notes C and E to fill out the chord and make it sound fuller. Either way, it's still C–E–G, no matter how you slice it. When you analyze a chord, you look for the basic notes that define it. Typically, they are not all in a pretty little row, in triadic order; many times you have to hunt around, but you can do that later on. Now you need to define exactly what makes each chord what it is.

Notable

If you understand your intervals well, building chords is no big deal. Each of the four triad qualities (major, minor, diminished, and augmented) has its own distinct building patterns, much as all the scales did. Once you learn the triad structures, you'll realize that they're so different from one another that it's hard to confuse them.

MAJOR TRIADS/CHORDS

Your First Harmony

The formations of each chord and triad are going to be described differently than in the past. Previously, it was formula first and then application. This time, you know enough to look at a chord first and then deduce the formula (with a bit of guidance). Start by looking at a plain C major triad. See the following figure.

Here's what you know about triads: they are three-note chords built in thirds. So, look at the structure of the intervals (which you know are thirds) between the notes and figure out the pattern.

First up is the interval of C to E, which is a major third. Next is E to G, which is a minor third. You can now form formulas for major triads: Start with a root, any root you want, and add a major third from the root and a minor third from the resultant note. Think of it as major3/minor3 for short, knowing that with triads, you are always dealing with third intervals, and this will give you the fast way to spell this triad.

AN ALTERNATIVE VIEW OF MAJOR TRIADS

Besides looking at the intervals in thirds, it is helpful to see a few other relationships that are present in the simple C major triad. First, look at C to E, which is clearly a major third interval. Now look at the interval from C to G. Intervals measure distance, and while the chord is composed of thirds, you're looking at the relationship only from one note to its adjacent note in the triad. What if you measured each interval from the root of the chord? Well, you would need to look at the distance from the first note (C) to the last note (G). The interval from C to G is a perfect fifth. To construct triads solely from the root, follow these steps:

1. Form a major third interval from the root of the chord.
2. Form a perfect fifth interval from the root of the chord.

It's important to know both ways to form triads. It's also beneficial to learn intervals from the root because you will realize something new: Triads have roots, thirds, and fifths!

Notable

Just like scales have to have seven notes and those seven notes have to use one letter from the musical alphabet each time they are spelled, triads must contain a root, a third, and a fifth. All the basic triads from C will contain some form of C–E–G (with different accidentals, of course), but all C triads will have C–E–G. Knowing this fact makes spelling triads much faster—especially when you learn the derivative approach to forming triads from each other (which you will get to very soon).

The other thing to know about major triads is that they also have the root, third, and fifth from the major scale that they come from. For example, if you're spelling a D major chord, just take the first, third, and fifth notes from the D major scale (which you know how to spell so well now)—D-F♯-A—and bingo, you have an instant major triad.

MINOR TRIADS/CHORDS

The Other Common Triad

Let's start with a C minor triad as in the following figure.

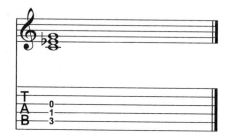

Based on what you know about intervals, look at the distance between each of the third intervals to deduce a formula for this triad. Start with C to E♭, which is an interval of a minor third. E♭ to G is an interval of a major third. So the formula would be a minor third, major third. If you compare this formula with the formula for a major triad (major third, minor third), you see that both the major triad and the minor triad contain a major third and a minor third. What's unique is that both triads contain one of each quality of third, but they are backward. The major triad is major third, minor third, whereas the minor triad is minor third, major third.

Notable

Here's a great way to remember the order of thirds in simple major and minor triads: The name of the triad will tell you the quality of the first third. Major triads start with major thirds, and minor triads start with minor thirds. Both triads conclude with the opposite interval; that is, major triads start with major thirds but conclude with minor thirds, and minor triads start with minor thirds but conclude with major thirds. Memorize this!

AN ALTERNATIVE VIEW OF MINOR TRIADS

You can also look at the minor triads in a few other ways to aid your understanding. First, look at all the intervals from the root of C:

- The interval from C to E♭ is a minor third.
- The interval from C to G is a perfect fifth.

Remember that the major triad also has a perfect fifth. This characteristic is yet another reason that it is called a perfect interval. Since the fifths don't change, you have to look at the thirds to find the differences between the major and minor triads. Major triads have major thirds, and minor triads have minor thirds, and both have perfect fifths from their roots. It's amazing that the difference between a C major triad and a C minor triad is just one note, yet they sound so different.

Here's another look at the derivative approach to music: If you can spell any major triad, all you have to do to make it into a minor triad is to lower the third of the major triad one half step. It's a trick that always works. Many times, your speed at working with theory can come from changing things you already know. If you memorize the major scale and the major triad early on, changing one note to make either one major or minor isn't such a big deal.

The third way to look at a minor triad is to relate it to its corresponding minor scale. Remember, the major triad took the first, third, and fifth note from the C major scale. The C minor triad does the same thing, just from its corresponding minor scale. To spell a C minor triad, spell the C minor scale and select its first, third, and fifth notes: C–E♭–G. This may or may not be the fastest way for you to work.

OTHER TRIADS

Diminished and Augmented

There are two other triads that are rarely used in modern music but are still important to know: the diminished triad and the even more unusual augmented triad.

DIMINISHED TRIAD

First let's look at the diminished triad. The following figure shows a C diminished triad.

Break down the intervals in the C diminished chord. Start with the interval from C to E♭, which is a minor third. The next interval, from E♭ to G♭, is also a minor third. The intervallic pattern of this triad is minor third, minor third. This is important to note, because both intervals are minor thirds. Both the major and minor triads contain one of each third (one major third, one minor third), albeit each triad had the thirds in different order. The diminished triad has the same thirds (both minor). Think of it this way: Each triad contains two thirds, and there are only major and minor thirds to choose from. You can have two triads that use one major third and one minor third (in reverse order), and that gives you two possible triads (major and minor). If you use the same third twice, you can get two more triads. In the case of using two minor thirds, you get a diminished triad.

Notable

The major, minor, and diminished triads occur naturally in music because of their relationship to scales. The final triad, augmented, is not a naturally occurring triad from any major or minor scale.

An alternative way to look at diminished triads is to look at all the intervals in the C diminished triad, all measured from C:

- The interval from C to E♭ is a minor third.
- The interval from C to G♭ is a diminished fifth.

The diminished triad is the first time you see a fifth in a chord that isn't perfect. That could explain why the diminished triad has an unusual sound when compared to the major and minor triads.

Although there is a diminished scale, most musicians don't correlate the spelling of a diminished triad to that of the diminished scale, even though the first, third, and fifth tones of that scale can be used to form the chord. The reality is that you probably won't deal with the diminished scale except theoretically, unless you are a jazz improviser.

AUGMENTED TRIADS

So far you've seen triads formed from almost every possible combination of thirds; all that's left is the augmented triad. The following figure shows the intervallic formula of a C augmented triad.

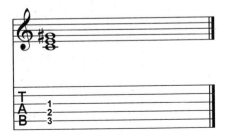

If you break down the chord by its third intervals, from C to E is a major third interval, and from E to G♯ is a major third. At last, you have every possible combination of thirds. The following table explains what you can do with three notes and two thirds; these are all the possible combinations of major and minor thirds in a triad.

TABLE OF TRIAD FORMULAS

TRIAD	FORMULA
Major	Major third, minor third
Minor	Minor third, major third
Diminished	Minor third, minor third
Augmented	Major third, major third

Diminished and whole-tone scales are considered symmetrical because they contain either the same intervals (whole tone) or the same repeating interval pattern (diminished). Since diminished triads are composed solely of minor third intervals, they are symmetric triads. Likewise, the augmented triad is symmetric because it is composed solely of major thirds.

Let's take another look at the augmented triad, this time from the root of C. The interval from C to E is a major third. The interval from C to G♯ is an augmented fifth. This is the second triad that has a nonperfect fifth (the other was diminished). It's also not a coincidence that the fifth is an augmented fifth and the triad is called an augmented triad (the same with the diminished chords, diminished fifth interval).

Using the derivative approach for forming augmented triads, if you start with the C major triad (C–E–G) and compare it to the C augmented triad (C–E–G♯), you come to the following conclusion: to make any major triad into an augmented triad, simply raise the fifth note one half step.

THE FULL DERIVATIVE APPROACH
FOR FORMING TRIADS

The derivative approach presupposes an ability to spell a major triad with ease. If you can't spell a major triad easily, practice until you can. Much of the theory in this book derives from the major scale in some way, simply because it's an excellent base.

The first slight change is that now you are only using numbers. So, instead of talking about the root, third, and fifth, you will say 1-3-5.

Here is a list of all the triads and how they derive from the major triad:

- Major: 1-3-5
- Minor: 1-♭3-5
- Diminished: 1-♭3-♭5
- Augmented: 1-3-♯5

This figure shows all the triads side by side so you can see what's happening musically.

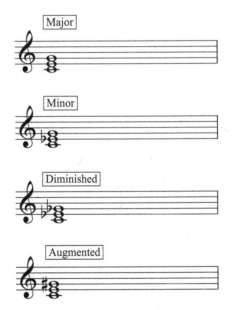

CHORDS IN SCALES

Making Triads

Scales are very important. They are an essential building block in music. Let's revisit the C major triad in the following figure.

This triad can be constructed in a few different ways. First, take the first, third, and fifth notes of the C major scale and stack them together to build a quick C major triad. This trick works in every major and minor scale, so in theory, you could build any major or minor chord you need. Since chords are built from third intervals, it would make sense that you could do more than just stack the first, third, and fifth notes. There are many possible third combinations in a scale if you start on each note in the scale and build triads. What would happen if you stacked these different combinations from each note? You'd get a lot of different chords, seven to be exact—one from each degree of the scale.

To learn how to make triads from every note in a C major scale, start with a C major scale and simply add triads (roots, thirds, and fifths) from each note in the scale. What you've just done is created all the basic harmonies (and chords) in the key of C major by creating triads off each note. See the next figure.

MUSIC THEORY 101

Don't downplay the significance of this accomplishment. You've just learned the basis for understanding harmony and chord progressions. Contained within those triads are seven different chords and endless possibilities for creating music. When you create triads from a scale and use only those notes to do so, you use a technique called diatonic harmony.

Now let's take a look at exactly what chords are created from making these triads (see the following figure).

| CMaj | Dmin | Emin | FMaj | GMaj | Amin | B° | CMaj |

You can see from the example that a variety of triads are created. There is a major chord, minor chords, and a diminished chord. Strangely, augmented triads are missing.

THE ORDER OF TRIADS

The order of triads in the scale is important. In a major scale/key, the triads always progress in this order: major, minor, minor, major, major, minor, and diminished. Memorize this order; it will serve you well—and the best part is that what you've just done in the key of C major holds true in every major key. Since all major scales are constructed in the same fashion, with the same intervals, when you stack triads in any major scale, you always get the same order of triads/chords. This is a huge time-saver! Only the names of the notes change because no two keys have the same pitch. The chords and their order will always be the same.

The next figure shows an example of this order of triads in the key of D major, B♭ major, and E major. The figure illustrates that no matter the scale, the same order of triads always exists. Just as major scales have formulas for their construction that allow you to spell any scale easily, knowing that the triad order holds true to all the keys is a dependable element in music theory.

Notable

Notice that the notes in the scales are in different keys, but the order of chords (major, minor, minor, major, major, minor, and diminished) stays the same. This holds true for every major scale/key.

ROMAN NUMERALS

To music theorists, there isn't any real difference between any major key. Unless you have perfect pitch—meaning you can name a note just by listening to it—you won't be able to hear a difference between C major and D major scales. Since there is such equality in the keys, music theory has a system of naming chords relative to the note of the scale from which they are built. If you were to number the notes and their corresponding triads from the G major scale, you'd end up with the image in the following figure.

Since triads are built off the notes, they can be referred to by a number and/or Roman numeral. For example, a one chord in the key of C major is the chord built off the first note in the scale, which is C major. Since every major scale starts with a major triad, the one chord in any major key is major.

The only limitation is that there is no way to convey whether that chord is major or minor simply by using the number 1, 2, or 3. Musicians use Roman numerals instead of Arabic numbers for this very reason. By using uppercase Roman numerals for major chords and lowercase Roman numerals for minor chords, musicians have created a system that makes sense in every key and conveys a lot of information about a chord.

Notable

Roman numerals are a standard way for music theorists not only to name chords, but also to analyze choral structures in pre-existing music in order to gain some insight into how the music was constructed. Roman numerals are still a convention in classical music. If you plan to study music formally, you need to know Roman numerals.

The next figure shows the harmonized major scale with the corresponding Roman numerals. Notice that the diminished chord is denoted by a lowercase Roman numeral and a small degree symbol next to it. That's the standard way to indicate diminished chords.

SEVENTH CHORDS

Seven Steps Away

As mentioned earlier, a triad is a three-note chord. Triads take care of most of the basic harmony, but not all of it. You build all chords in thirds. When you derived diatonic harmony from major and minor scales, you stacked thirds from each root and came up with seven triads—all built in thirds. Your knowledge of intervals allowed you to decode what the triads were and in what order they appear. See the following figure.

Now, what would happen if you added another third to your triads? Well, simply, you'd form seventh chords, which are so named because the last interval added is seven notes away from the root. You could call them quad-ads, but it doesn't have the same ring to it as seventh chord does—plus it sounds like a form of sit-ups.

Notable

The majority of the harmony you deal with is built in intervals of thirds. This type of harmony is called tertian harmony and is the basis for common practice or tonal harmony that is studied and still utilized today.

DIATONIC SEVENTH CHORDS

The term *diatonic* means "from the key." You first learned about diatonic when you formed simple triads within a scale. Do it again in F major.

Now, to make these diatonic triads into seventh chords, add another third on top of each triad, adding an interval of a seventh if you measure from the root. Remember to use only the notes from the F scale (F–G–A–B♭–C–D–E–F) when adding your thirds to keep this example diatonic. Doing so will leave you with these seventh chords (see the following figure).

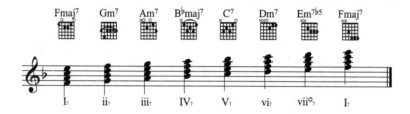

In this list, there are four different types of seventh chords: major seventh, minor seventh, dominant seventh, and half-diminished seventh.

Notice that in the previous figure, the Roman numerals used to analyze the chords did not identify which kind of seventh chord it was. They simply added 7 next to each Roman numeral. The answer had to be spelled out. So you need to understand what makes a major seventh different from a dominant seventh, even though both use uppercase Roman numerals (signifying major chords) with sevenths attached to them.

Notable

Even if your experience with theory is limited, you've probably come across, played, or heard about a G7 chord (or any other root). This is one kind of seventh chord (as you will learn about). This book uses the term *seventh chord* as a broad category. Seventh chords come in many different types, and G7 is simply one type.

SEVENTH CHORD CONSTRUCTION

Seventh Chord Blueprints

This section explores all the available seventh chords. A seventh chord is nothing more than a triad with an added seventh interval (when measured from the root). This gives you at least eight seventh chords (four possible triads and two sevenths), although there is one more that breaks the rules.

MAJOR TRIADS WITH SEVENTHS

To make a major triad into a seventh chord, there are only two possibilities: a major triad with a major seventh on top, and a major triad with a minor seventh on top. Start with the following figure.

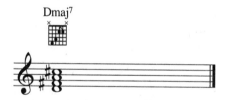

When you look at this chord, you can see two things: a major triad (D–F♯–A) and an added C♯. The interval from the root of the chord to the seventh (D to C♯) is a major seventh. Call this chord a major/major seventh chord for a second because it tells you exactly what you have: a major triad with a major seventh interval added. Now, the rest of the world calls this chord a major seventh, as in D major seventh, or Dmaj7 for short. Many theorists use major/major seventh to be more specific, but if you say D major seventh, you're saying the same thing. The major seventh chord is found on the first (tonic) and fourth (subdominant) degrees of a harmonized major scale.

You could think of the formula for a major seventh chord as being 1, 3, 5, 7. (This is if you take the scale degrees from a major scale.)

Notable

The major seventh chord is interesting for two reasons: First, you can spell it simply by choosing the first, third, fifth, and seventh notes from any major scale. This is because a major seventh chord is the tonic seventh chord in a major key. Second, its proper name of major/major seventh shortens to simply major seventh.

The next possible seventh chord is shown in the following figure. Looking at this chord, you see another D major triad (D–F♯–A) and an added seventh of C. The interval between D and C is a minor seventh. This chord is called a major/minor seventh chord. When it's shortened, it's called a seventh chord, as in G7, or D7 in this case. The term *seventh chord* is far too general for music theory. Theorists and many musicians call this chord a dominant seventh chord because it occurs only on the fifth scale degree, which has the proper name of the dominant scale degree. Whichever you call it, G7 or G dominant seventh, both are correct.

The formula for a dominant seventh chord is 1, 3, 5, ♭7 (if you take the scale degrees from the major scale). Dominant seventh chords are important. It's hard to have harmony without dominant (V) chords.

MINOR TRIADS WITH SEVENTHS

Minor triads with sevenths also have two varieties. Look at the next figure.

Start with a C minor triad (C–E♭–G) and add a B♭. The interval from C to B♭ is a minor seventh, so this chord is called a C minor/minor seventh chord. It's shortened to C minor seventh, Cm7, or C-7. This is the basic minor seventh chord that is found on the second, third, and sixth scale degrees of a harmonized major scale. Again, just as the major seventh, when both the triad and the seventh are the same (both minor), the name of the chord is simply minor seventh. You can form the minor seventh chord by taking the first, third, fifth, and seventh notes from a pure minor scale (Aeolian). If you wanted to relate the scale to major, its formula would be 1, ♭3, 5, ♭7 (relating the scale degrees to the major scale).

The next seventh chord is the first unnatural seventh chord; it's not formed in the diatonic major or minor scales. Take a look at the next figure.

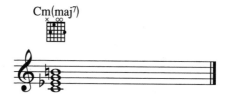

This C minor triad with an added B natural gives a very unusual sound—unnatural, even. The interval from C to B is a major seventh, so the full name for this chord would be a C minor/major seventh chord. There is no other name for this chord. The only shorthand you may see is in the chord symbols in popular music: Cm(maj7), C-(maj7), or Cmin(maj7). While these chords have an unusual sound, they can be quite striking when used in the proper context. Again, this triad does not occur anywhere in the natural major or minor scales.

A formula for a minor/major seventh chord would appear as follows: 1, ♭3, 5, 7 (if you take the scales degrees from the major scale).

DIMINISHED TRIADS WITH SEVENTHS

Diminished chords are a bit tricky, especially when it comes to naming them. Start with the diatonic diminished seventh chord (see the next figure), built from the leading tone of a major scale.

What you have is a B diminished triad with an added A. The interval from B to A is a minor seventh, so the full name for this chord is a diminished/minor seventh. However, here's where it gets tricky. This chord is called a half-diminished chord. Half-diminished chords use the symbol B⌀7.

A formula for the half-diminished seventh chord would look like this: 1, ♭3, ♭5, ♭7 (if you take these from the major scale degrees).

This chord, while it may be the diatonic chord, is not the typical diminished seventh chord. Look at another diminished seventh chord in the following figure, which explains why that particular chord is called half diminished.

Start with a diminished triad and add an A♭. The interval from B to A♭ is a diminished seventh. The full name for this chord would be a diminished/diminished seventh. Just like major and minor seventh chords that share the same name and type of seventh, this is the diminished seventh chord. It's also called a fully diminished seventh chord, but for most people, diminished seventh will do. The symbol for a fully diminished seventh chord is B°7.

A formula for the diminished seventh chord would look like this: 1, ♭3, ♭5, ♭♭7 (if you take these from major scale degrees). Note: this is the first time you've seen a double flat in a chord formula. Fully diminished seventh chords don't occur in major or minor scales naturally; they are the result of stacking minor third intervals. You can also derive this chord if you harmonize the harmonic minor scale at the leading tone degree.

HALF AND WHOLE DIMINISHED

Why is one diminished chord half diminished and another whole diminished? Well, for starters, it's a name. But there's more to it than that. The diminished triad is a symmetric chord in that it uses all minor third intervals. When you spell a diminished seventh chord, you actually use all minor thirds again (B–D–F–A♭). It is called fully diminished because it follows the pattern of all minor thirds and becomes perfectly symmetrical at that point. A half-diminished chord (B–D–F–A) has a major third between the fifth and the seventh and isn't fully diminished because it loses the pattern of all minor thirds. That's where the difference comes from. Usually when you see diminished chords with sevenths, they are fully diminished seventh chords. Half-diminished chords are used mostly in jazz.

Since the diminished chord comes in two flavors, modern musicians differentiate these two chords. Look at a half-diminished chord as a minor seventh chord with a ♭5: To avoid confusion, most modern music uses min7b5 instead of the half-diminished symbol (⌀). This way, when you see a diminished symbol (°), you can infer that it's a fully diminished chord.

AUGMENTED TRIADS WITH SEVENTHS

Augmented triads have a particular sound that isn't used very much. Nonetheless, modern music, especially jazz, uses augmented seventh chords, which come in two varieties. Start with the following figure.

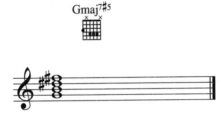

Start with the G augmented triad of (G–B–D♯) and add an F♯. The interval from G to F♯ is a major seventh, so this chord would be called an augmented major seventh. For short, the symbol G+(maj7) or Gaug(maj7) is used. A formula for this chord would look like this: 1, 3, ♯5, 7 (if you derive this from the degrees of a major scale).

The other augmented chord is shown in the next figure.

Start again with the G augmented triad and add an F. The interval from G to F is a minor seventh, so the full name for this chord would be an augmented minor seventh. Typically, this is shortened to G+7, Gaug7, or G7♯5. The G+7 chord is closely related to a G7 chord. The augmented nature of the raised fifth is simply seen as an alteration.

The formula for this chord would look like this: 1, 3, ♯5, ♭7 (if you derive the formula from major scale degrees).

SEVENTH CHORD RECAP

The following table contains all the formulas side by side.

FORMULAS DERIVED FROM A MAJOR SCALE

NAME	SYMBOL	INTERVALS
Major seventh	Cmaj7	1, 3, 5, 7
Dominant seventh	C7	1, 3, 5, ♭7
Minor seventh	Cmin7	1, ♭3, 5, ♭7
Minor/major seventh	Cmin(maj7)	1, ♭3, 5, 7
Half-diminished seventh	C⌀7	1, ♭3, ♭5, ♭7
Fully diminished seventh	C°7	1, ♭3, ♭5, ♭♭7
Augmented major seventh	C+(maj7)	1, 3, ♯5, 7
Augmented seventh	C+7	1, 3, ♯5, ♭7

Chapter 7

Chord Inversions and Progressions

Chords are more than just a collection of intervals. To understand chords in their entirety you need to look at a few more aspects including chord inversions and progressions. Understanding chords and how they are spelled is only the first step. Once you can look at a chord and give it a name, you need to look for context. What chord preceded this one and what comes after? Are there patterns to observe? This chapter contains the answers to all these questions as you study how chords move from one to another.

INVERTED TRIADS

Mixing Things Up

When you think of the word *inverted*, what comes to mind? Most people think of upside down or backward. When it comes to inverted chords, this is actually not too far from the truth. Every triad and seventh chord you have seen in this book has been in "root" position. Root position means that the root of the chord (the tone its name is derived from) is the lowest note in the chord. Although there are a lot of times when chords appear in root position, it's not the only way that they function. Any other note in the chord can take the lowest voice, and that is exactly what an inversion is: when the third, fifth, or seventh note (if present) is in the bass voice. With inverted chords comes a new set of symbols.

Let's start off with the root position C major triad (see the following figure).

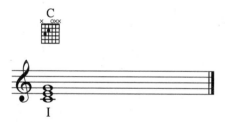

By now you should be able to identify this chord quickly as a root position C triad. Go a step further and analyze it with a Roman numeral. The answer is Roman numeral I, because in the key of C, C is the tonic or I chord.

Now, to start inverting this triad, raise the bass note (which is C) one octave. The result is the next figure.

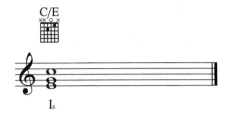

I_6

With the C raised an octave, the third of the chord (E) becomes the lowest-sounding note in the chord. Whenever the third of the chord is in the bass (the lowest-sounding) voice, that triad is said to be in first inversion. Now, there are two ways to name this chord: the classical way and the modern way.

The classical way of naming this triad would be to call it a I_6. Why is it called a I_6? If you look at the interval between the lowest note in the chord (E) to the C, it is a sixth; that's where the 6 comes from. The interval from the E to the G is disregarded because it's a third and it's accepted that it would be a third. That is just the way it has evolved.

When analyzing this chord in classical style, every first inversion chord will have a small subscript 6 next to its Roman numeral. This is true no matter what kind of triad it is; major, minor, diminished, and augmented in first inversion are all 6 chords. It also doesn't matter which Roman numeral they are functioning as. All seven chords in the harmonized scale can be in first inversion with the marking of a subscript 6.

Now, as to the modern notation, this one is easy: The triad is simply called C/E, which translates to C chord with an E in the bass. The slash (/) is commonly referred to as "over," as in triad over bass note.

Remember how the first inversion was made? You simply took the lowest note and popped it up one octave. Well, to get to a second inversion, you are going to do exactly the same thing. This time, you start with a first inversion triad and move the E up an octave. The result is shown in the next figure.

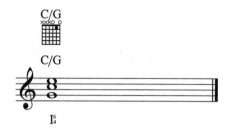

That wasn't so hard to do, was it? So, to summarize what you have now: You still have a C triad and the notes C–E–G; those elements never change. What has changed is that the lowest note in the chord is now the fifth of the chord (G). Whenever the fifth of the chord is in the bass of any triad, it becomes a second-inversion triad.

The classical way of naming this triad would be to call it I_4^6. It's an I_4^6 triad because the intervals from the lowest note (G) are as follows: G to E is a sixth and G to C is a fourth, so that's where $_4^6$ comes from.

Notable

In baroque times, harpsichordists read inverted chords written as figured bass. Figured bass was basically a bass note and a bunch of numbers under the notes. Based on the numbers present, the player would know what chord to play and in what inversion, very much like the modern jazz guitarist or pianist who reads off a lead sheet.

A modern musician would see that chord as C/G, which is defined as a C triad with G as its lowest note.

Since triads have only three notes, you are all out of inversions. Here's what you've learned about inversions:

- If a chord is in root position, no further action is necessary.
- If a chord is in first inversion (the third of the chord is in the bass), it is called I_6 or C/E (depending on the triad; C is just an example).

- If a chord is in second inversion (the fifth of the chord is in the bass), it is called I$^6_4$ or C/G (if C triads are used as examples).
- Any triad, regardless of its type—major, minor, augmented, or diminished—can be inverted.
- Every chord in the harmonized scale can be inverted, so every Roman numeral from I to VII can be inverted using the figured bass symbols for first and second inversion.
- If you see a Roman numeral with nothing after it, it is in root position.

INVERTED SEVENTH CHORDS

One More Inversion

In theory, inverted seventh chords are no different from triadic inversions. However, a seventh chord has one extra note, so you get one more possible inversion: the third inversion. The other difference is that the classical music theory figurations that name the inversions are completely different for seventh chords. Other than that, the same rules apply.

You're going to use the G7 (G–B–D–F) chord in the key of C, so this chord functions as a dominant, or V, chord.

In root position, nothing changes, so there's nothing to show, it's simply G7 or V.

The first inversion of a G7 chord moves the G up an octave, placing the B in the lowest voice (see the following figure). This inversion is specified with the symbol V_5^6. You could also call this chord G7/B, or G seventh with B in the bass.

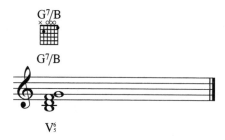

The $_5^6$ may seem confusing, but it's not really. There is a sixth from B to G and a fifth from B to F.

The second inversion puts the B up an octave, leaving the D as the note in the bass (see the next figure). The inversion is specified as a V_3^4 chord. The fourth is from D to G and the third from D to F. This chord could also be called G7/D, or G seventh with D in the bass.

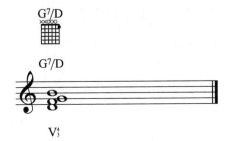

V_3^4

The third inversion of a G7 chord places the D up an octave, leaving the seventh of the chord, F, in the bass (see the following figure). The figuration of this chord is called a V_2 chord. The 2 is there because the interval from F to G is a second (since everything else in the chord is thirds, you don't need to list them).

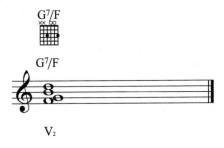

V_2

This chord could also be called G7/F, or simply G seventh with F in the bass.

Notable

Here's an easy way to remember the inversion configurations of a seventh chord. Start with $^6_5$ for a first inversion, $^4_3$ for a second inversion, and 2 for the third inversion. The numbers descend from 6: 65–43–2. That's easy to remember, right?

Here's a recap on seventh chords:

- If a seventh chord is in root position, no further action is necessary.
- If a seventh chord is in first inversion (the third of the chord is in the bass), it would be called a V^6_5 or G/B (depending on the chord; G is just an example).
- If a seventh chord is in second inversion (the fifth of the chord is in the bass), it would be called a V^4_3 or G/D (if G is used as an example).
- Any seventh chord, regardless of its type—major, minor, augmented, or diminished—can be inverted.
- Every seventh chord in the harmonized scale can be inverted, so every Roman numeral from I to vii can be inverted using the figured bass symbols for first, second, and third inversion.
- If you see a Roman numeral with nothing after it, it is in root position.

CHORD PROGRESSION

From Here to There

Simply put, a chord progression is a movement of chords from one point to another. If you've ever heard a blues song, you've heard a progression of chords. All the pop music from the last one hundred years is loaded with chord progressions. If you play guitar or piano, you know all about chord progressions. The trick now is to figure out what they are, why you need to know them, and, more important, how this information is going to help you.

CHORD STACKS

When you studied how to make chords, you looked at the chords a few ways. First, you stacked diatonic notes from the scales and ended up with seven different chords. You also dissected the intervallic properties of every triad and seventh chord in existence. This is one way of looking at chords. But there is another angle. When you talk about chords as vertical stacks of notes, you essentially are adopting a philosophy that chords are objects.

Notable

Chords and melodies are tied together very tightly. When you play a melody, you can almost imagine what harmony is present with that melody. As a result, it's possible to think melodically and harmonically at the same time. Beyond the theoretical underpinnings of what melody notes fit with which chords, when you listen to a melody, that melody has a way of telling you what chord it wants to have accompany it—all you have to do is listen.

THE CHICKEN OR THE EGG?

The concept of vertical stacks works pretty well in studying a single chord. Looking back through the development of music shows that chords, although they are vertical stacks of notes, are closer to being vertical collisions of voices. What does this mean? Well, imagine that you are not playing guitar or piano; you are in a choir. There are soprano, alto, tenor, and bass voices. At the simplest level, there is one singer per part. Is a person in the bass section singing one note at a time, singing chords? No, he's singing a line—a melody, to be more specific. Since one voice can't make a chord, you have to look at the net result of what the choir is singing. There are four melodies going on at once. Each part is different. Now, if you freeze any single slice of vertical time, you could look at all the notes that are sung on the first beat of the first bar and come up with a chord. That would make sense because music should sound rich and consonant, and chords and harmony allow this. Now ask yourself which came first, the individual lines of music or the chords? Did the voices simply flesh out the chords as they went along?

The answer is complicated. It's hard to say for sure because most of the composers are dead. However, throughout the development of music, especially classical music, lines ruled and chords were afterthoughts.

Put simply: composers wrote lines of melodies that summed together as chords when musicians looked up at them (vertical thinking). Since music theory has a wonderful ability to look back at composed music, it's easy to forget that lines were dominant.

Using the tools of music theory, you can look back at any piece of music, new or old, and figure out what chords are used and why. The better question to ask is why. Why did anything happen the way it did? Why did Bach use certain chords and not others? Why did Beethoven and Mozart use similar chords? Were they working from some sort of rule book, so to speak? The answer is no. Harmony developed. It's as simple as that. Diatonic harmony was a long time in the making. It started with one voice, then a second was added, and so on, and then eventually triads and harmony fell into place. It wasn't until the baroque era that harmony started to solidify into something recognizable. The music evolved because musicians listened and studied what had come before. They took what they liked and moved forward.

Notable

Theorists look back and try to fit all the music into a set of rules. But this is not always in your best interest. It is worth noting that a certain sequence of chords happens over and over and over again, but trying to figure out why will drive you crazy. In the end, you'll understand that there are sounds associated with feelings, moods, and other things that cannot be quantified with theory. Remember: music first, theory second.

DIATONIC PROGRESSIONS AND SOLAR HARMONY

The Center of the Musical Universe

The logical place to begin is with progressions that are purely diatonic (coming from the major or minor scales). Just using the chords from the diatonic major scale can make a lot of music. The next figure illustrates the key of D major and its chords.

In the key of D, any of these chords are acceptable for use, since they are made exclusively from notes in the D major scale (just stacked together).

Now, you're looking at seven different chords—some major, some minor, and one diminished. Which ones do you choose and why? Well, first start out with a concept, and then explore the chords you see most often.

In any musical key, the tonic, whether it's a note or a chord, carries the most weight and importance. So, you could say that the "one" chord is the center of your universe, and you'd be right. In harmony, especially traditional tonal harmony, the tonic is a point of resolution. Music typically, if not always, comes back to that one chord.

The analogy about the tonic chord being at the center of your universe is going to serve your musical imagination well. Imagine that the one chord is at the center of the solar system; it's the sun. All the other chords rotate around that central chord with different degrees of pull (more on that later). This concept is called "solar" harmony and it's an accepted way to look at chords. The tonic chord is really important, just like the sun.

PRIMARY CHORDS

In a major key, there are three primary chords, which are the basic chords used to spell out and harmonize the key. The primary chords in any major key are I, IV, and V.

Amazing Grace

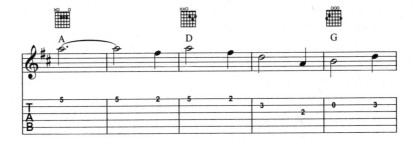

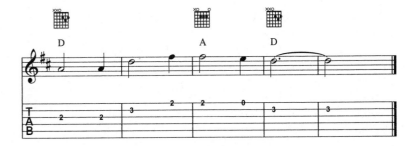

Not coincidentally, all three of the primary chords are major. Now, what can you do with just primary chords? The majority of folk music, sacred music, all of blues, and a good chunk of rock are based on primary chords. Ever heard the phrase *three-chord rock*? Well, those are the three chords. For an illustration, look at a song most people know, "Amazing Grace," in the previous figure.

This is an example of a lead sheet. For ease of reading, this song was kept in D major. The melody is on top and the chords are listed only by symbol. For the benefit of the guitar players, chord grids were put in. A piano player would have to realize the chord voicings on his or her own, but this does not change the fact that this simple folk melody is properly harmonized with the three primary chords from its home key.

This is the first step to analysis. The key signature tells you D major or B minor, but the existence of D, G, and A chords tells you that you are in the key of D major because those chords—I, IV, and V—are the primary chords for D major.

The primary chords can go a lot further; they are not relegated to pop and folk music. Classical music makes heavy use of primary chords—all tonal music does.

Three chords will get you only so far, so you need to look a bit deeper into the scale to see what else you can find to use.

SECONDARY CHORDS

In addition to the I, IV, and V chords, you have the secondary chords in the key. The secondary chords are the ii, iii, and vi chords in any major key.

As you can see from the lowercase Roman numerals, all three chords are minor. Once you know what chords are diatonic to a key, just remember that the primary chords are the major ones and the secondary chords are the minor ones.

Is music written with only secondary chords? Not often, although there are almost always some rule breakers. The secondary chords embellish the primary chords and give chord progressions variety.

Here is an example of a simple chord progression with no melody (see the next figure), which contains voicings for piano and guitar using both primary and secondary chords in the key of A major.

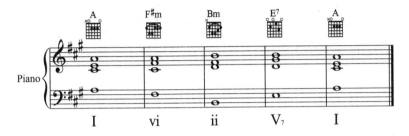

As you can see in the example, this progression flows well. This example uses only chords that are diatonic to the key of A major and while the result may not rock the world of music, it's a nice-sounding chord progression.

The key point here is that chords aren't chosen at random. There are some nicely established norms when using chords. The first step is to understand how to use diatonic chords and how to write with them. Afterward you can explore, through analysis of other music, exactly how far outside the lines you can color, so to speak.

Notable

Look at the two examples of chord progressions in this chapter. Notice anything? Well, to start, each progression starts and ends on the tonic chord. The penultimate (second-to-last) chord was a V chord in each case. Is this merely an accident, or do V chords precede I chords at the end of a progression (also called a cadence)? You'll just have to read on to find out for sure.

Now, here are some typical ways that chords progress from one to another. You're going to study solar harmony and the almighty chord ladder.

SOLAR HARMONY

Musical Gravity

Earlier in this chapter we touched briefly on solar harmony by stating that the tonic chord is the most important chord in any key and that the other chords circle around it. Now you'll discover what this actually means.

Notable

Although there are seven diatonic chords available, there is no steadfast rule about which one to use and why. However, it is possible to study the evolution of music and see some trends that are worth investigating, even if you choose to go off in your own direction and look at chords differently.

In tonal music, the tonic chord serves two roles: the start and the end. It begins phrases and ends them. The term *gravity* is hard to explain on paper, but you know it when you drop something on the floor. With musical gravity, when you write tonal music, progressions tend to gravitate back to the tonic chord each time. Because phrases tend to want to come to rest and end there, composers worked their hardest to prolong the inevitable moment of coming back to the strong tonic. Eventually, tonality in classical music fell out of favor because too many composers found the strong tonic chord increasingly difficult to use in new ways. Amazingly enough, to this day, tonal music thrives, and harmonic gravity gives music its power and beauty.

The following figure gives a good example of tonal gravity.

Isn't that brutal? Doesn't that F♯ want to pull up to the G more than you can express? Why does it do that? No one knows for sure, but you have hit on exactly what makes melodies and chord progressions move: the inevitable pull back to the tonic note. You saw it with a simple melody; it appears in the next figure with a single chord voicing.

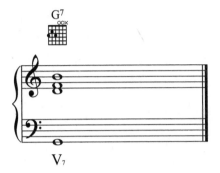

Why is it that this chord refuses to sit still? This chord, a G7 chord, is diatonic to the key of C major. It is the V chord, or dominant chord. In this example, it is a seventh chord. So, why does this chord want to go someplace else? Harmonic gravity. It's not the tonic chord; it's actually one step removed from it. It's the closest chord to tonic (more on that soon), and it wants to go to tonic. The next figure shows how it resolves.

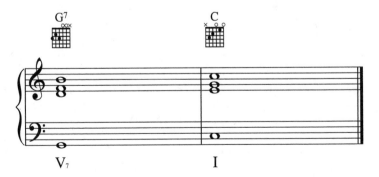

You came back to the tonic, back to the center of the musical system, and finally you have resolution. Tension and release are what make this whole game work.

You've heard about two chords: I and V. Now, look at the rest of the chords and how they align with the tonic chord by looking at the chord ladder.

THE CHORD LADDER

Step on Up!

The chord ladder is a neat little device that shows the relationships among all the diatonic chords in a key. Take a look at the ladder in the following figure, and then you'll learn more about exactly what it's showing you.

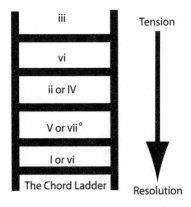

It's a ladder with chords on it. Basically this ladder is a reference to the "harmonic" gravity mentioned earlier. All the chords in some way fall to the I chord at the end.

There are a few things to observe. First, notice that there are different steps on the ladder, and occasionally there is more than one chord on those steps. When two chords occupy the same step on a chord ladder, it means that the chords can substitute for each other. Before you go any further, you need to know what makes a chord substitute for another chord.

CHORD SUBSTITUTIONS

On the first step of the chord ladder is the I (tonic) chord and a very small vi chord on the final step. They occupy the same step because both chords can substitute for each other. They share common tones; more specifically, they share two-thirds of their tones. In the key of C major, I and vi share the following tones (see the following figure).

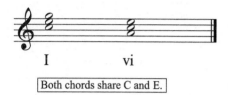

I   vi

Both chords share C and E.

On every step of the ladder, when you find two chords occupying the same place, it's because they can substitute for each other due to sharing of tones.

LADDER OF FIFTHS

Remember the circle of fifths? Here's a ladder of fifths. Many, many chord progressions are based on movements of fifths. So, now look at the chord ladder without the extra chords and view it as strictly fifth-based movements from the tonic chord up (see the next figure).

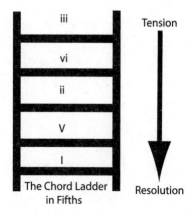

The Chord Ladder in Fifths

You end up with a progression of iii, vi, ii, V, I. Look at that for piano and guitar in the next figure.

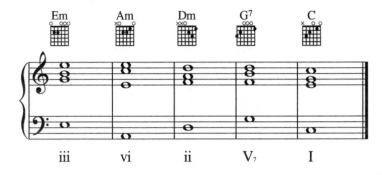

This example sounds fine, doesn't it? Sure it does!

Now start to throw in some of the substitute chords, as in the following figure. See what replacing the ii with a IV and the V with a vii° chord look and sound like.

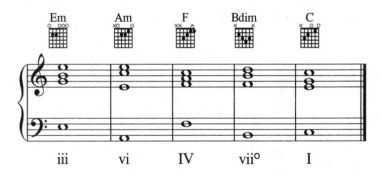

You get a nice-sounding progression. Unfortunately, no matter how you slice any of these progressions and no matter how crafty you are, when you get to the V (or its substitute, the vii° chord), you pull back to I. Or do you? Remember the small vi chord next to I on the chord ladder.

DECEPTIVE RESOLUTIONS

The small vi chord is there as a deceptive resolution to the I chord. Essentially, you break the pattern that V has to resolve to I by allowing V to resolve to vi. It's called a deceptive cadence.

Here's what so neat about the progression: Just when you think you're going to cadence back to I and essentially end the progression, the music pulls a fake out and gives you a vi chord. It prolongs the progression as it sets you back a bunch of steps on the ladder, giving you more time to keep the musical phrase alive and continue the progression.

If you wondered why the vi chord was in very small print, that's because while it substitutes for the tonic chord, it's more of a transport, magically linking you back to the real vi chord on the chord ladder. Maybe the ladder should have looked like the following.

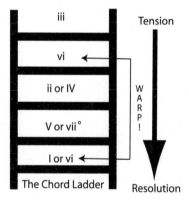

Notable

The chord ladder does not dictate what you should or should not use when writing music. It simply presents a number of choices that will work well together. The ladder illustrates how chords typically progress in diatonic situations. Feel free to use it as a starting point and go your own way from there.

Chapter 8

Exploring Harmony

The past few chapters dealt with chords; now it's time to learn about melody. Understanding how chords and melody are related will complete your knowledge of harmony. Chords never exist alone and melodies can't survive without chords to support them. You have learned about scales and how they make melodies. You have learned about chords and their origins. You have studied how chords progress from one to another, but it's time to learn how melody and harmony relate to each other.

MELODY

Steps in the Right Direction

You have studied so many elements of music in this book, and yet you have never asked this simple question: What is a melody? Well, there is a good reason for not broaching this question—it's really hard to answer.

At its simplest, a melody is the tune of a song. Sing "Happy Birthday" to yourself. You just sang the melody. That was easy because that particular song is practically all melody. What does all melody mean? Well, in the case of "Happy Birthday," while there may be some chords behind it, they're not necessary; the tune stands on its own with or without chords. The melody is the memorable part, not the chord progression.

Now, for some contrast, listen to a Beethoven symphony and try to sing the melody. That's going to be harder because a symphony is not as clear-cut! There are multiple melodies going on at once. So, why go to all this trouble? The relationship between melody and harmony is crucial to the study of music theory. No matter how well you understand scales and chords, if you don't understand how they relate to one another, your knowledge will be incomplete.

SUPPORTIVE CHORDS

Let's use a simple analogy to explore the relationship between melody and harmony. Chords are like ladders, supporting melodies. At its simplest, a single melodic tone can be harmonized with a chord as long as the chord has the melodic tone in it.

So, if you are in the key of C major, you have a melody note C, and you want to figure out what chord would work with that note, look to the key of C major and its harmonized chords. Then select a chord that had the note C in it. Now you have the three choices shown in the following figure.

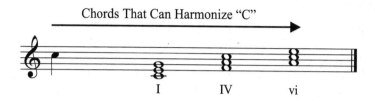

Chords That Can Harmonize "C"

I   IV   vi

The chord you choose depends upon a few variables. You could listen to each chord and select the one you want. However, you're dealing with one moment in time, and you'd probably want to see the context that this note occurs in throughout the piece, taking into account chords that precede and follow it.

At the most basic level, a single note is supported by a chord that shares the same note. If you've ever wondered why "insert any chord here" is being used at any moment, look to the melody; it will always be related in some way.

Notable

When harmonizing single notes, remember that the chord you choose will contain the melody note as either its root, third, or fifth. If you stick only with simple triads, you will always have three choices. Add a seventh chord and you have four choices for chords. It's nice to have choices.

POINT FOR POINT

As you start this process, learn how to harmonize a scale point for point, meaning that each note of the scale gets its own chord. Each melody note has at least three choices for chords, which leads to a staggering number of choices. Rather than list them all, here is an example (see the next figure) that will work well here. Instead of choosing random chords, the chord ladder was the starting point, and the rest of the chords were selected by ear.

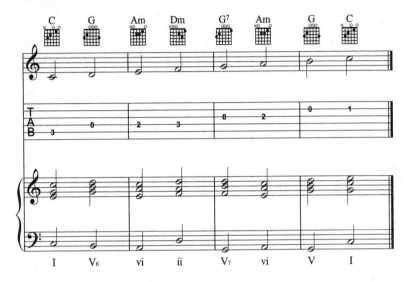

This illustration gives you an idea of how to choose chords for melodic tones.

Does every melody note get its own chord? Not always. The truth is that not every note in a melody needs to be harmonized with a chord of its very own—that would definitely be overkill.

Notable

Look at the sheet music to any pop song you like. You will see that 99.9 percent of the time, chords support several melody notes. There is almost never a new chord for each melody note unless the melody is very, very slow—at which point the harmony is keeping the song from sounding like a dirge.

CHORD TONES AND PASSING TONES

Making Harmony Work

The interaction of chords and melodies centers on one basic point: chord tones or passing (nonharmonic) tones. In the following figure, the chord tones are highlighted and the passing or nonchord tones are printed normally. Compare the harmony to the melody, and you will see many different points of similarity. In general, for a harmony to work for any given melody, the majority of the melodic tones should be contained in the chord that supports it. There is no steadfast rule of how many tones per bar, but for music to sound consonant, the melody needs to line up with the harmony enough times to make the listener feel as if they're in the same key. A passing tone does not necessarily have to move by step to and from a chord tone, but if you think of the odds, a triad has three notes and a scale has seven, you're most likely using a passing tone as the triad takes three-sevenths of the scale with it and leaves three of the other four tones as passing tones. Only one tone will exist as a true nonharmonic tone, but then again, it may sound just fine.

Amazing Grace

Notable

You're back to thinking vertically again, which is good. It's important to see the effect of harmony against melodies and vice versa. It's a bit of the chicken-or-the-egg question. Just don't forget to listen and play each example so that you can hear and not just think about the music. Certain things won't make much sense on paper but will work wonderfully as you listen.

KEY CONTROL

One of the nice things about melodic harmonization is your ability to set up the keys you'd like to use. When looking at a single-note melody, it's almost impossible to tell whether you're in a major or a minor key unless you have some harmony to support it. When you start with just a melody, you can control the mood of the piece by choosing either the major or the related minor key. Since any melodic tone can be taken by at least three different chords, you can control your keys very closely.

Here is a simple example, using a key signature of no sharps and no flats, which could be either C major or A minor. The example uses a whole-note melody over a few bars. Look at the melody by itself in the following figure.

Although a melody could apply to either key that the key signature supports, there is one thing that could sway it to the minor key. Remember the leading tone? In the key of A minor, the G♯ is a telltale sign that the piece is in the key of A minor. The melody stayed away from that—completely on purpose—as that would have locked the music into that key.

Getting back to the example, since the G was avoided, look at the next figure to see how this could become a C major melody.

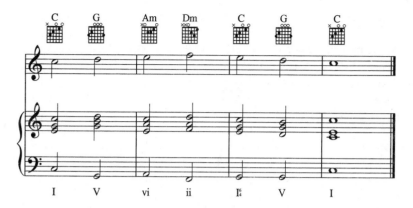

Simply by choosing chords from the key of C, making sure to throw in the all-important dominant V chord, establishes the key of C major. There might have been a chord ladder used, but it was more of a process of elimination at a piano or guitar to see what chords fit best with the notes written.

Now, to push the piece in the direction of A minor, just use chords from the key of A minor and make sure that it has its own dominant V chord—in this case, E7. The next figure shows the result.

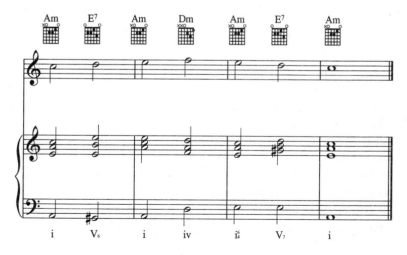

CHORD TONES AND PASSING TONES

By sticking to A minor chords and typical progressions in that key, it is pretty easy to transform this basic melody into an A minor melody. It's amazing that a simple melody has to be defined by its chords, but this is the general balance that must be followed: Melodies and harmonies rely on each other. Neither one can exist solely on its own.

Notable

One of the coolest things you can do with harmony is take a phrase of music (like the example), harmonize it in one key, and then at some point in the piece, harmonize it in another key. That process will give the same melodic material some contrast and another flavor. It will allow you to reuse good material without making it sound stagnant.

TRUE MELODIC HARMONIZATION

What Notes Work Where

Let's move on to another aspect of melodic harmonization that doesn't have to do with harmony. Think of a few musical acts that use harmony; for example, Simon and Garfunkel and the Beatles. These groups use true melodic harmony: notes that sound consonant with each other. You've no doubt heard some bad attempts at harmony, usually at holiday parties after a few glasses of spiked eggnog. Someone tries to sing a second part to "Silent Night" or some other tune. The result is usually less than desirable.

It's important to have a general idea of what notes work when harmonizing single-line melodies. This is how chords evolved. Gregorian chant started with a single line of music, called monophony. As time went on, a second voice was added. Limited intervals were allowed, usually fourths and fifths (hence they are called perfect). Over many hundreds of years, a system of harmony built on thirds evolved. This system, known as tertian harmony, has been the focus of this book because it is the basic formula for harmony. Since tertian has as its root tertiary or three, thirds are a great place to start.

ONE THIRD FITS ALL

The first place to look is thirds. Simply put, you can spot harmonize any melody by harmonizing a diatonic third above the original melody.

The diatonic part is key here. You can't just play any third (major or minor); you have to know what key the melody is in and play the notes that fit with it. The next figure gives a very simple example in D major.

To harmonize this melody, start a second part, three notes up in the D major scale, and follow the contour of the original melody. The result is shown in the next figure.

The second line is harmonized a 3rd above.

INVERSE

The inverse of a third is a sixth, and a sixth is another very nice way to harmonize a melody. Typically, you'd harmonize a sixth down, diatonically. This brings you to the same notes that you had when you went a third up. The difference is that the harmony is now below the original melody note. Both approaches work well. Check out the first example, this time with parallel diatonic sixth harmony, in the following figure.

The second line is harmonized a 6th below.

INTERVALS YOU CAN USE

When harmonizing, certain intervals work almost all the time, and others are very hard to use. Here is a list of the intervals by type. Remember that when you are harmonizing melodies in keys, think diatonically for the melody notes.

- **Unison/octave:** Not really a harmony per se, but the effect of doubling a melody can be a nice way to add some textures.
- **Seconds:** Seconds verge on the edge of tension and dissonance and should be handled with care. They can work at certain points in a harmony for some color, but you'll rarely find more than one in a row; you can forget parallelism.
- **Thirds:** You can't go wrong with thirds. They just always sound nice. They work great in parallel too.
- **Fourths:** Fourths can be nice, but not in parallel. Parallel fourths are one of the major no-no rules of voice leading. However, since there is a fourth interval from the fifth of a triad to the root, a fourth can be just the right interval.
- **Fifths:** Fifths are also consonant intervals that work well. You don't want them in parallels either as they break the other major rule of voice leading. Plus, if you harmonize with straight parallel fifths, it will sound like Gregorian chant.
- **Sixths:** Sixths are the inverse of thirds. Sixths also always sound very good all the time. They work in almost all situations, especially in parallel motion.
- **Sevenths:** They are another dissonant/tense interval. They may work at certain points, but in general, sevenths won't sound consonant. You're also rarely, if ever, going to see them in succession one after another.

In general, the tense intervals, the seconds and sevenths, are not something to avoid. A bit of tension and release is what music is built on, so using those intervals sparingly may add just the perfect color to your music.

Notable

Historically, when harmonizing notes, composers had to be especially careful with voice leading, moving notes in parallel with each other (where one voice follows the exact shape of the original melody). Thankfully, thirds are always nice when used in parallel motion.

SINGLE-LINE HARMONY

Go Across

Harmony has been the domain of chordal instruments throughout this book. Sure, a clarinet in an orchestra contributes to a sense of harmony in terms of the whole score, but how can all the single-line instruments (ones that can play only one note at a time) get in on this party? (There are more single-line instruments than chordal instruments.)

An arpeggio is a chord played one note at a time. Play enough arpeggios and you end up with chords. They aren't chords in the vertical sense, as single-line instruments can't play that way, but they are harmony—more specifically, implied harmony.

The good news is that if you play a single-line instrument, you've probably already played harmony this way. Many of you didn't even know that you played implied harmony. The next figure gives an example.

Since the arpeggios are labeled and named with Roman numerals, you can clearly see that harmony is definitely going on here. It's simply moving across the page instead of up and down.

Single-line harmony is an unavoidable part of playing tonal music. Think of it this way: Everything starts as scales. Scales combine to form chords, which in turn form harmony. It's almost impossible to write music without being aware of harmony and its implications. Music for single-line instruments would be boring without some sense of harmonic implications. The music would wander without purpose.

Notable

If you want to see single-line harmony, here are a few places to look: the solo cello suites by Bach (and his flute and violin solo works too) and concertos by Vivaldi, Mozart, and Beethoven. Those are the well-known ones. Every instrument has some principal composers; for example, Rodolphe Kreutzer is known exclusively as a violin composer.

JAZZ AND JAZZ HARMONY

Uniquely Beautiful and Complex

Jazz is a young genre of music that continues to evolve and reshape itself at a breathtaking pace. Jazz is categorized by several important elements. One is instrumentation: bass, piano, drums, saxophone, and trumpet come to mind. The other is improvisation. It's actually the strongest component of playing jazz: improvising melodic solos over chord changes. It's one of the things that truly sets jazz apart. Let's look at the elements of jazz as they relate to music theory.

JAZZ HARMONY

Jazz harmony is unmistakably rooted in the tradition of music theory. It relies on melodies that are harmonized with chords. The principal difference between jazz harmony and other harmony is its use of chords that are taller than triads—taller as in vertically, on the page, like the G13 chord shown in the next figure.

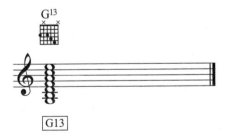

The G13 chord is considered a tall chord because it's tall on the page. It fits into a class of chords called extended chords. To understand extended chords, you need to understand extended intervals. This book's earlier discussion of intervals didn't say much about extended intervals, but jazz harmony requires it. You need to know what a thirteenth really is and what extended intervals are.

Notable

Jazz is one of the few purely American art forms that do not directly come from the European tradition. Instead, it was slowly formed from its origins in gospel music and the blues music of the Deep South. It quickly grew through the great jazz innovators such as Louis Armstrong, Miles Davis, Charlie Parker, and John Coltrane, to name a few.

EXTENDED INTERVALS

By now, intervals should be a common part of your music theory experience. Intervals have shown you the exact distance between any two notes. Up until now, you have not distinguished intervals larger than an octave.

Let's do a quick review: After you pass the octave (which is also called an eighth), you distinguish these larger intervals with, you guessed it, larger numbers. Any interval larger than an octave is considered an extended interval. However, there are some intervals that are never extended.

Music theory does not distinguish the distance of a third or a fifth differently, no matter what octave it is in. Much of this has to do with historical practice, but the real reason lies in triadic harmony.

Notable

Since the majority of jazz chords include extended intervals, just remember the rule of nine in order to decipher what a ninth from C is, for example. In jazz, the seventh chord is the smallest unit you will see, and typically taller chords are more common than seventh chords, so you'll need to know extensions in order to succeed.

If you start stacking thirds on top of one another, you get this order: C-E-G-B-D-F-A-C. Or as intervals: root, third, fifth, seventh, ninth, eleventh, thirteenth, and root.

Using the rule of nine from Chapter 2, the extended intervals (ninth, eleventh, and thirteenth) spell the same as a second, fourth, and a sixth; they are just an octave away. The reason you don't see tenths and seconds (thirds and fifths) is that when you stack thirds, those intervals simply don't come up. Once you get to thirteen, the next third brings you back to the octave.

The other reason that thirds and fifths are not counted as extended intervals becomes clear when you hear them compared to other intervals (such as seconds versus ninths). To most ears, thirds and fifths sound the same no matter what their octave. This is not to say that they sound identical, but the difference is so minute that you don't need another name for them based on whether they are more than an octave apart. A second sounds very different than a ninth. Try this out on your instrument.

EXTENDED CHORDS

You learned about four families of chords: major, minor, diminished, and augmented. When sevenths are added into the equation, you get a fifth chord family: dominant chords (major triads with minor sevenths). These basic five chords and their extensions make up the majority of jazz harmony. To get by in jazz, you need to understand major, minor, and dominant extensions first. You will deal with diminished (which is typically note extended) and augmented chords later.

EXTENDED MAJOR

The basic jazz major chord is the major seventh chord. As you recall, a major seventh chord is a major triad with a major seventh interval added to it. In addition to the seventh, you see major chord extensions.

Major chords can be written the following ways and still fall under the umbrella of major and, thus, substitute for each other:

- C Major 7th
- C Major 9th
- C Major 11th
- C Major 13th

The formula for these chords is pretty simple to spot: root (major) extension. Any chord that follows that formula is in the major seventh family. For example: F Major 9th is a major seventh chord, but F9th is something else because it lacks the necessary major component in its name. Knowing these basic rules will make life much less confusing, as jazz deals with chord symbols more often than actual written voicings. That's right, in jazz, you turn symbols into sounds.

In jazz, all major chord extensions take their notes from the major scale built off the root. A D Major 13th chord will take all of its notes from the D major scale. This is important because the spelling of the individual notes has to follow the home scale or the chord won't sound right. In practice, advanced jazz musicians often alter the notes in very tall chords, but that's a matter of personal taste.

EXTENDED MINOR

The basic jazz minor chord is the minor seventh chord. As you recall, a minor seventh chord is a minor triad with a minor seventh interval added. In addition to the seventh, you see minor chord extensions. Minor chords can be written the following ways and still fall under the umbrella of minor and, thus, substitute for each other:

- C minor 7th
- C minor 9th
- C minor 11th
- C minor 13th

The formula for these chords is pretty simple to spot: root (minor) extension. Any chord that follows that formula is in the minor seventh family. For example: F minor 11th is a minor seventh–type chord, simply extended.

In jazz, all minor chord extensions take their notes from the Dorian scale built off the root. A D minor 13th chord will take all its notes from the D Dorian scale. This is important because the spelling of the individual notes has to follow the home scale or the chord won't sound right. In jazz, the home scale for minor chords is the Dorian mode, not the expected natural minor scale.

EXTENDED DOMINANT

The basic jazz dominant chord is the dominant seventh chord. As you recall, a dominant seventh chord is a major triad with a minor seventh interval added to it. In addition to the seventh, you see dominant chord extensions. When used in practice, many jazz players will simply call these chords seventh chords and leave off the moniker dominant as it's implied. Dominant chords can be written the following ways and all still fall under the umbrella of dominant and, thus, substitute for each other:

- C7th
- C9th
- C11th
- C13th

The formula for these chords is pretty simple to spot: root extension. Any chord that follows that formula is in the dominant seventh family. For example: F11th is a dominant seventh–type chord, simply extended to the eleventh.

Typically, with dominant chords comes chordal alterations. An alteration is some sort of change to the fifth or ninth of the chord. An altered dominant chord may read like this:

- C7♭9♯5

Even though that chord looks kind of scary, it's still plainly dominant because at its core, it's a C7 with other stuff added to the end of it.

In jazz, all dominant chord extensions take their notes from the Mixolydian scale built off the root. An E13th chord will take all its notes from the E Mixolydian scale. This is important because the spelling of the individual notes has to follow the home scale or the chord won't sound right. In jazz, the home scale for dominant chords is the Mixolydian mode, not the major scale (that's reserved for major seventh chords).

JAZZ PROGRESSIONS

Grounded in Tradition

Jazz players used songs from the Great American Songbook as vehicles for jazz improvisation. They played the melodies instrumentally (or sang them if a vocalist was involved) at the start of the tune; this is called playing the head of the tune. Once that was done, the chords that formed the harmony of the song remained while the soloist improvised a new melody; this is called blowing on the changes. At the end, they'd play the melody one last time and that was it.

Because jazz players favored these songs so much, their melodies and harmonies became the foundation for jazz harmony. These songs became the songs that all jazz players know and play today; they are aptly referred to as standards. The harmonies of these songs have some regular patterns that appear over and over again, and thankfully can be studied. Start with the diatonic progressions.

THE DIATONIC PROGRESSIONS

In jazz, if you simply take the diatonic major scale and harmonize each chord up to the seventh, you can learn a lot about how jazz harmony functions. The following figure shows the A♭ major scale harmonized in seventh chords.

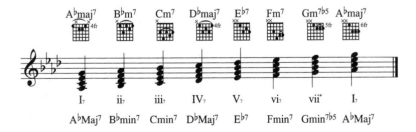

You'll be happy to learn that the basic jazz progressions are diatonic and still follow the chord ladder. Start with the mighty jazz progression of the ii–V–I.

In jazz nothing is more common than the ii–V–I progression. Look at the next figure.

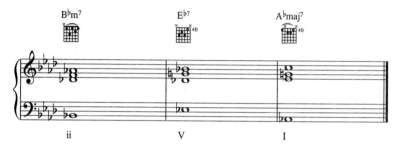

If jazz harmony were distilled to one central point, it would be the ii–V–I progression. It's simply all over jazz music. Sure, it gets more complicated, but the ii–V–I is the basic harmonic unit that all jazz players use.

What's interesting is that a ii–V–I is a substituted IV–V–I (as ii and IV substitute for each other), which is just a I–IV–V (remember those simple primary chords) reordered. Why change the IV to ii? By doing so, you create three different chords: a minor seventh chord, a dominant seventh chord, and a major seventh chord. That made jazz sound different from other styles of music.

Add some extended chords and you get a very distinctive jazzy vibe out of this progression. See the following figure.

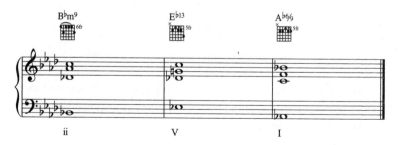

Add a few more chords before the ii and you reach the other common jazz progression, the iii–vi–ii–V–I. See the next figure.

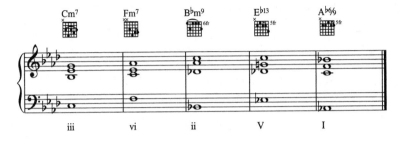

MINOR PROGRESSIONS

There is a minor key equivalent to the ii–V–I progression in major. It's still a two–five–one, but the qualities of the chords change. Instead of Dm7–G7–Cmaj7 (in the key of C major), the progression becomes Dm7♭5–G7–Cm7 (see the following figure).

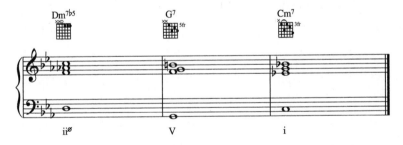

This progression is easy to spot because you also have three distinct chords, with a dominant chord in the middle. Look for the min7♭5—that's usually the signpost that screams, "Hey, minor two five coming"—and see if the chords that follow it line up.

Now, look at how a real jazz tune is put together. The next two figures present a common standard without the melody, just the changes (jazzspeak for the chords).

Fmin⁷   B♭min⁷   E♭⁷   A♭Maj⁷

vi   ii   V   I

A♭Major _____

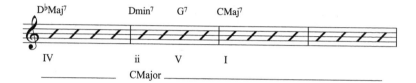

D♭Maj⁷   Dmin⁷   G⁷   CMaj⁷

IV   ii   V   I

_____ CMajor _____

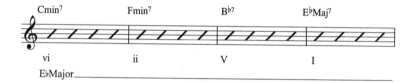

Cmin⁷   Fmin⁷   B♭⁷   E♭Maj⁷

vi   ii   V   I

E♭Major _____

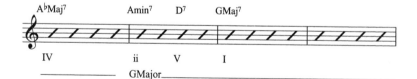

A♭Maj⁷   Amin⁷   D⁷   GMaj⁷

IV   ii   V   I

_____ GMajor _____

Amin⁷   D⁷   GMaj⁷

ii   V   I

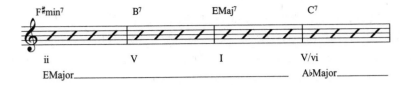

F#min⁷ — B⁷ — EMaj⁷ — C⁷

ii — V — I — V/vi

EMajor_____ A♭Major_____

Fmin⁷ — B♭min⁷ — E♭⁷ — A♭Maj⁷

vi — ii — V — I

D♭Maj⁷ — D♭min⁷ — Cmin⁷ — B°⁷

IV — iv — iii — iii°

B♭min⁷ — E♭⁷ — A♭Maj⁷

ii — V — I

Notice the analysis under the chords. There are loads of ii–V–I progressions in many keys, both major and minor. This is standard practice for jazz (changing keys often), but beyond that the progressions are fairly simple; it's just modulating often.

Notable

The previous figure is essentially a lead sheet. This skeletal form of music tells you what chords to play on what beats and, if a melody is present, the melodic line. If this figure had a melody, it would be enough for an entire band. The chords would be created from the symbols, the bass player would walk a bass line that made sense with the chords, and the melodic players would improvise on the chord changes.

BLUES FORMS AND HARMONY

12 Bars of Perfection

Now that you have heard about chords and harmony, it's time to cover the blues, a basic ingredient in jazz. Jazz grew from the blues and still relies on the blues as a standard form and song style. The blues is just plain cool. The blues exists in two varieties: minor blues and major blues. Each blues song is exactly twelve bars (or measures) long. Blues songs follow a strict repeating harmonic formula, so it's easy to transpose them into any key, and in general they are easy to learn to play.

12-BAR MAJOR BLUES

The 12-bar blues is taken from the traditional blues you might hear in the blues clubs or by someone like B.B. King, but jazz players have adapted the harmony just a bit. Take a look at what a traditional 12-bar blues piece looks like in the following figure.

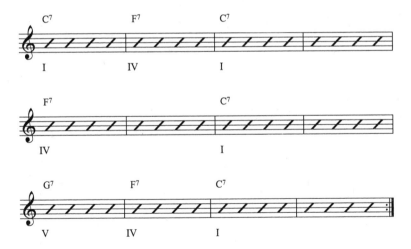

Now, contrast that with the blues that most jazz players play, shown in the next figure.

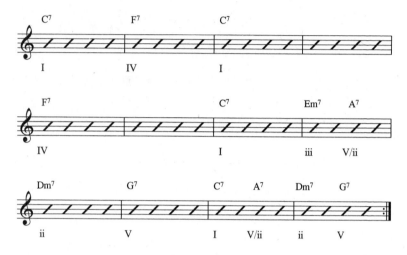

The last five measures are where you see a change. Instead of the traditional blues V–IV–I ending, the standard jazz ii–V–I progression is thrown in. Preceding that ii chord, a V/ii is thrown in to set up the progression and make life a bit more interesting for the improviser.

Notice how the Roman numeral harmony, chord symbols, and guitar chords are given for each example. This way, you can transpose the chords into any key. The B♭ blues is definitely one of the most used, standard jazz/blues keys, so it's a good one to start with.

Here's a list of jazz tunes that are based on the 12-bar major blues:

- "Now's the Time" (Charlie Parker)
- "Blue Monk" (Thelonious Monk)
- "Straight, No Chaser" (Thelonious Monk)
- "Billie's Bounce" (Charlie Parker)
- "Tenor Madness" (Sonny Rollins)

There are a million more, but this will get you started. Make sure to transpose them into different keys. If you don't play harmonies, learn some melodies (all the jazz blues have heads, so learn those).

12-BAR MINOR BLUES

The final variant of jazz blues is called the minor blues, and you guessed it, it's in a minor key. Take a look at the minor blues in the following figure.

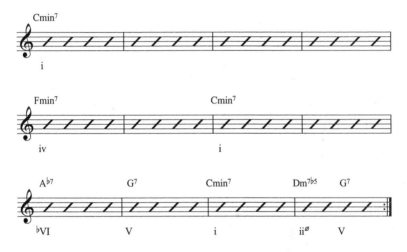

You see some basic harmony, such as i and iv chords, and the expected dominant V chord that you need for minor keys. The chord that is slightly off is the ♭VI chord that precedes the V chord in bar nine. That's simply what makes a minor blues work the way it does; it is a definite difference between the major and the minor.

Notable

If you're looking for jazz tunes to play, check out a "real book," which is a takeoff on the "fake books" that include melodies, basic chords, and lyrics so musicians can improvise with any song. There are tons of real books available, and each is a repository of hundreds of jazz lead sheets with melodies, words, and chord changes. It's a great place to study and learn some great music.

Also, you'll notice a turnaround in the last bar of a Dmin7♭5, G7. This turnaround sets the i chord up in bar one so the tune can loop around. The progression is the minor version of a ii–V–I progression.

Chapter 9

Reading Music

Music is more than just notes and rhythms. Opening up any piece of music reveals other symbols and markings that are crucial for making music. For the composer, these additional symbols convey exactly how the music should be played and organized. Elements such as tempo, dynamics, bar lines, and repeat symbols have their own specialized markings—and many of these are in another language!

Italian is the most common written language of music. The majority of music uses standard Italian language symbols. Depending on the nationality of the composer, you may run into other languages. German composers sometimes write markings in German, French composers in French, and so on. If you run into these often, pick up a foreign language dictionary and look up every term in the music. Don't miss a vital clue because you didn't take the time to look up a word. Certain instruments deal with other languages more often than others. Classical guitarists, for instance, often play music of Spanish composers who mark up their music in Spanish.

TEMPO

The Speed of Your Music

So far you have learned a lot about how to read the basic symbols of music: pitch and rhythm. Yet, at this point, your understanding of music is still basic, and many other symbols exist to reproduce flat two-dimensional symbols into rich three-dimensional music. Tempo markings are one such element.

Rhythm deals with the duration of pitches. The duration of those rhythms depends on the tempo of a piece. Tempo is defined as the speed of your musical beat. In the case of $\frac{4}{4}$ time, tempo governs how fast the quarter notes are. Tempo is a vital factor in music and is expressed a few ways: either numerically or in general Italian markings that have been in use for hundreds of years. You may have heard that using a metronome can help keep your rhythm intact. It's time to learn more about how a metronome can help you.

Metronomes

A metronome is a simple device. The metronome, invented around 1815, has one simple job: to keep time without speeding up or slowing down. The first metronomes used a mechanical pendulum-type design that clicked from side to side. Metronome speeds are based on how many times they click per minute; this is also referred to as beats per minute, which are expressed numerically. All metronomes allow you to set their speed based on beats per minute, usually ranging from 40 beats per minute (a slow tempo) up to 200 beats per minute (a fast tempo). Beethoven was a staunch supporter of the metronome when it came out because it allowed the composer to signify exactly how fast a composition should be played. The metronome survives today because it is an effective tool for practicing music. Metronomes exist in two varieties: mechanical designs that you wind up and electrical designs that work on a battery.

Numerical Tempo Indications

Music written after 1815 may have numerical tempo indications that correspond to metronome markings. Composers give you the exact speed of the music and you set your metronome to that speed and play. Most modern music has metronome marks.

As you can see in the following figure, the metronome marking is numerical and is shown with the note that receives the beat. In $\frac{2}{4}$, $\frac{3}{4}$, and $\frac{4}{4}$, typically the quarter note is counted, since the quarter note receives the beat in simple time. In $\frac{3}{8}$, $\frac{6}{8}$, $\frac{9}{8}$, and $\frac{12}{8}$ you set the metronome to count dotted quarter notes (every three eighth notes). As you know, compound meters are typically felt in groups of three notes. Instead of setting the metronome to count individual eighth notes, set the metronome to the dotted quarter (which is three eighths!). In the case of cut time ($\frac{2}{2}$), the metronome is typically set to the half note. In short, the metronome is set for the pulse of your song, which varies for each meter and each piece.

Expressive Tempo Indications

Before the age of metronomes, composers spoke of time and tempo in broad terms. Since most musical terms are rooted in Italian, tempo markings are Italian words that suggest a range of tempos (or tempi). This style of conveying tempo is the oldest and most standard way to show tempo markings. While you don't need to learn the entire Italian language, many of the markings you'll see will be in Italian, so it's worth knowing them.

Here is a chart of all the common tempo markings and their corresponding metronome markings so you can set your metronome properly to practice. All the tempo markings are approximate ranges of tempo. Musicians often have their own ideas of what these terms mean, which is why the terms are so general.

TEMPO MARKING	WHAT IT MEANS	BEATS PER MINUTE
Grave	very slow	40 bpm
Largo	slow	50 bpm
Larghetto	not as slow as largo	55 bpm
Adagio	slow	60–70 bpm
Andante	moderately slow "walking tempo"	70–85 bpm
Moderato	moderate	85–100 bpm
Allegretto	not quite as fast as allegro	100–115 bpm
Allegro	fast	120 bpm
Vivace	lively and fast	140 bpm
Presto	really fast	150–170 bpm
Prestissimo	really, really, really fast	170+ bpm

Another thing worth mentioning is that most metronomes have tempo markings written on them as a guide to help you. When in doubt, take a look; your metronome most likely has the markings and the approximate settings already printed on it, in case you forget. In addition to the standard tempo markings, there are a few words that modify the tempo to give a bit more direction. Here is a list of the standard terms you may encounter.

- a poco a poco (little by little)
- assai (very)
- molto (much)
- con (with)
- meno (less)
- non troppo (not too much)
- più (more)
- pochissimo (a very little)
- poco (a little, somewhat)
- quasi (almost like, sort of)

For example, if you see allegro non troppo it means fast, but not too fast. Composers use these terms to suggest the speed and mood of a piece. Certainly, numerical tempo indications are the clearest of all, but composers still choose to use text to convey the general idea, allowing the individual performer some freedom to interpret. Listen to a few different versions of the same piece of classical music; you'll hear variation in the tempi of the pieces, among other things.

Notable

No matter what form of tempo markings you are using, tempo markings appear at the beginning of a piece, above the first measure, usually just to the right of the clef. Tempo can be reindicated at any point in the piece if it should change.

Ritardando, Accelerando, and Other Terms

So far, the tempo markings you've learned have related to the overall speed of any particular piece. But music is not a static thing and neither is tempo. There are times where you want to speed up the music a little and times when you want to slow it down a little. These instances don't need a full tempo change, especially when the changes are very subtle and short-lived.

Ritardando, which means "to slow," is used to denote sections that need to slow down gradually. This is useful at the end of a section when most melodies naturally feel like slowing down. But you can find a ritardando anywhere in music. Ritardando can also be abbreviated as rit. The following figure shows a ritardando in action. As you can see, the ritardando is usually accompanied by a dashed line that extends under the note or notes that the composer wants you to slow down.

Accelerando is the opposite of ritardando: it means to speed up gradually. It is notated much the same way, with a dashed line extending under the sections. Accelerando is also often abbreviated as accel. The next figure shows both rit. and accel. in action.

There are a few more common terms that apply to tempo and tempo changes that you should know. Many of these are similar to each other; still, certain composers opt for some terms over others.

- rubato (elastic tempo; speed up or slow down at will)
- ritenuto (slow down suddenly)
- rallentando (slow down gradually; abbreviated as rall)
- più moso (a little faster)
- più lento (a little slower)
- a tempo (revert back to the piece's original tempo)

DYNAMICS

The Loud and Soft of It

Dynamics, and their corresponding dynamic markings, are responsible for telling you how loud or soft to play throughout a piece of music. Dynamics are a vital element of music. Pay attention to them when you read music—they are as important as the notes and rhythms! Dynamics are an inexact science, since each instrument can produce varying degrees of loud and soft. Again, just as with tempo indications, Italian terms are used to communicate dynamics. Dynamic markings are always abbreviated.

SIMPLE DYNAMIC INDICATIONS

In its simplest form, there are two basic dynamics: forte and piano. Forte, which means "loud," is represented as a single *f*. Piano, which means to play soft, is always represented as a single *p* (see the following figure).

Notable

Piano, isn't that an instrument? Pianos don't just play softly! The full name of a piano is a pianoforte because the instrument was capable of playing softly and loudly—something that other keyboard instruments, such as harpsichords, were not able to do.

If all you have is loud and soft playing, you won't be able to express a full dynamic range. There has to be some gray area and in-between dynamics. You can double and triple up on **p** and **f** to get extremely loud or extremely soft (see the next figure).

The Italian word mezzo, which means "in between," is a common word in music. When applied to dynamics, mezzo gives a few more dynamic options between piano and forte (see the following figure).

Now that you know all these dynamics, let's look at the progression of dynamic markings from the softest to moderate to the loudest sounds possible (see the next figure).

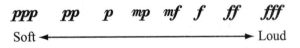

CRESCENDO AND DIMINUENDO

All the text-based dynamic markings you have learned so far have imparted sudden and immediate shifts in the volume of the music you're playing. Two symbols exist to show gradual changes in dynamics.

A crescendo, which is a wedge shape that opens to the right ——————————, instructs you to get louder. The length of the wedge corresponds to the length of the increase in volume. At the truncation of the wedge there will be a new dynamic symbol telling you how loud you should be at the end of the crescendo. Crescendos (or crescendi) are most often seen as wedges, but you might also see the word written out or abbreviated as cresc. (see the following figure).

A diminuendo is the opposite of a crescendo and is often called a decrescendo; they mean the exact same thing. Diminuendos (or diminuendi) instruct you to get softer via a wedge shape that is open on the left and gets smaller as it goes along ———————. Again, at the end of the diminuendo you will see what dynamic marking you should be playing. The diminuendo can be written out or abbreviated as dim. or decres. (see the next figure).

Another modifier to dynamic markings is sforzando, which means "a sudden strong accent." If your dynamic moves to sforzando, which is abbreviated as sf or sfz, play a strong, sudden forte. You can also combine sforzando and piano dynamics together to make an sfp, which would mean to play a sudden strong forte followed by a piano dynamic.

NAVIGATION IN A SCORE

Where to Go from Here

Music is typically read from left to right. However, there are symbols and markings that point out specific sections to repeat and play again. There is a navigation system that tells you exactly how to play a piece. The need for such a system lies in the fact that it's not easy to turn the page while you're playing music; most instruments require both hands to play.

SPECIAL BAR LINES

Bar lines do more than just break up the measures into easy-to-read segments; they also direct the player to stop or repeat the music. The first "special" bar line is the final bar line. A final bar line is necessary at the end of a section or at the end of the piece of music. It is simply a double bar line with a very dark outer line (see the following figure).

At the end of a section a composer may place a double bar line to indicate some sort of change. You'll find double bar lines whenever something in the music changes drastically (see the next figure).

REPEATS

The bar line can easily be transformed into a repeat marking. Repeat marks signify that a section, or even the whole piece, is repeated. Repeat bar lines come in two varieties: whole repeats and sectional repeats. A repeat symbol is simply a final bar line that has two dots. The simplest repeat sign is the whole repeat. A whole repeat will appear at the end of a piece of music. The dots face to the left (see the next figure), signifying that you should play the entire piece of music again.

Repeat to the Beginning

The arrow in the previous figure is there just to visually remind you where to repeat. In a real piece of music, you would only find the normal repeat markings, without the arrows.

The other variety of repeat symbol is the sectional repeat. A sectional repeat has two repeat bar lines, one at the beginning of the section and one at the end of the section. Whenever you see a repeat like this, you simply repeat the music between them. You'll notice in the next figure that the repeat bar lines are the opposite of each other: the beginning repeat has its dots facing right, while the ending repeat has its dots facing left. This indicates which section should be repeated.

Repeat Between the Bar Lines

If a certain pattern of notes or chords is repeated exactly the same way, you may see a measure repeat symbol: ✗. This symbol tells you to repeat the previous measure. If the repeat symbol sits on the bar line between two measures ✗✗, you are instructed to repeat the previous two measures. In long stretches where the music is identical, it's often less confusing to see these symbols instead of identical measures (see the following figure).

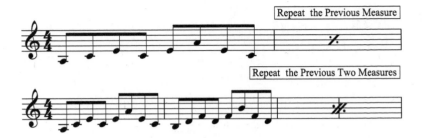

Repeat the Previous Measure

Repeat the Previous Two Measures

MULTIPLE ENDINGS

When traditional repeats don't fit into a particular situation, there are other options. One such option is the use of multiple endings. For example, suppose the music repeats a section of twelve measures and the composer wants you to play a different twelfth measure the second time you play it. Typically, a repeat sign works with exact sections only. For this example, the best option is to use multiple endings. In a multiple ending, traditional sectional repeat symbols are used; the only difference is that some measures are meant to be played the first time you play it and different measures the second time, most commonly called first and second endings (see the next figure).

Play up to the repeat sign the first time through.
On the second pass, when you reach the "1" (first ending) you skip everything under that bracket and play the measures under the "2" (second ending).

You play the music under the section labeled "1" the first time. When you repeat, you skip all the music under the "1" and go directly to the section labeled "2." You don't play the first ending again because you already have. There can be more than two multiple endings too!

Notable

Theoretically there can be as many endings the composer wishes, and the same rules apply. Keep repeating and playing the correct endings based on the number of times that you've repeated. Once you've finished the last repeat, you progress through the rest of the piece.

CODAS

A coda, which comes from the Italian term for "tail," is a section at the end of the piece. A coda is signified with this symbol: $\oplus$. A coda is basically a transport symbol. When you come to a coda symbol, you magically jump from the symbol to the coda section, which has a corresponding coda symbol. This coda section is always at the end of the piece. The first coda symbol may have some other instructions along with it, such as "second time only." Traditionally, coda symbols are grouped with D.C. and D.S. symbols, which you're going to learn shortly. This will clear up what codas are and how they are used.

D.C.

D.C., which is an abbreviation of da capo, literally means "to the head." The D.C. symbol is another way to signify that you should repeat a piece of music. When you come to a D.C. symbol, it means go back to the very beginning. It's often combined with other things, which are covered in the last section of this chapter.

D.S.

D.S., which is an abbreviation of dal segno, literally means "from the sign." D.S. markings always have an accompanying symbol, the sign or segno, which looks like this: $\%$. When you see a D.S., you simply repeat back to wherever the segno symbol is. This is like a sectional repeat, just written out differently. Usually D.S. markings are combined with other things, covered later in the chapter.

FINE

Fine, which literally means "the end," is used to denote a place to stop. What's special about a fine is that it's typically combined with other symbols, such as D.S. and D.C. Fine is used in a situation where you need to repeat back to the beginning or other part of the music and then stop in a particular spot other than the last measure. The fine command is usually ignored the first time you see it; its significance only becomes clear as you read farther along in the piece.

COMBINING SYMBOLS

Now let's combine the symbols. Coda, D.C., D.S., and fine are rarely seen alone. They are most often combined with each other to form instructions. The next four figures are all the possible combinations of D.C., D.S., coda, and fine in real musical examples.

As you can see from the example, most of the symbols—such as fine, ⊕, and 𝄋—rely on information later in the piece to activate them. The first time you read through the music, you can typically ignore these types of symbols. As you progress to more and more complex music, you will encounter one of the preceding combinations that will bring those symbols to life.

D.C. al Coda

D.C. al Coda

Read the first two lines until the

D.C. al Coda.

Repeat back to the start and play until the ⊕.

When you reach the ⊕

jump directly to the other ⊕ and finish.

Fine

D.C. al Fine

D.C. al Fine

Read the first two lines until the

D.C. al Fine.

Repeat back to the start of the piece

and end where it says *Fine*.

D.S. al Coda

Read the first two lines until the

D.S. al Coda.

Repeat back to the 𝄋 and play until the ⊕.

When you reach the ⊕

jump directly to the other ⊕ and finish.

D.S. al Fine

Read the first three lines until the

D.S. al Fine.

Repeat back to the 𝄋

and end where it says *Fine.*

Chapter 10

Expression Markings and
Other Symbols

As you advance to more difficult pieces of music, the music becomes more expressive. Playing the correct notes and the correct rhythms isn't enough. Composers strive to give exact information on how to play those notes. Through expression markings, composers can vary the attack and smoothness of certain notes. The rest of the common musical symbols help clarify the thoughts and sounds of music.

EXPRESSION MARKINGS

Add Dimension to Your Music

Without expression music would be flat and boring. You could feed a computer a musical score and it would play a perfectly executed piece of music. The notes would be correct and the rhythms would be perfect. What's missing are the subtle nuances that only human performers give to music. Music lives and breathes; it's not a static thing. While many performers naturally bring their own form of expression to each note they play, there is a system of markings that give specific information about exactly what to play—and more importantly, how to play it.

SLURS

A slur is simply a way to connect two notes smoothly. Every instrument gives life to a slurred note in a particular way. No matter how your instrument produces sound, when you play a note there is an "attack" to each note. A slur is a marking that tells you to smoothly connect those notes and lessen the attack as much as possible. On a wind instrument, this could mean not breathing between each note. On a violin it would indicate to use one long bow. It's different on each instrument. No matter what instrument you play, a slur marking always looks the same. It is a curved line that connects two or more different notes (see the following figure).

A slur looks suspiciously like a tie, and this is a common error. But actually, they are easy to tell apart (see the next figure): A tie is a curved line that connects two of the exact same notes. A slur is a curved line that connects different notes. Here is an example for clarity.

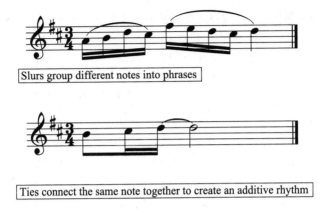

Slurs group different notes into phrases

Ties connect the same note together to create an additive rhythm

Notable

In terms of notation, slurs are typically drawn on the alternate side of the stems. If the phrase had stems that faced up, the slur would be drawn under the notes; if the stems faced down, the slur would be drawn over them—this is simply to avoid clutter.

LEGATO

Legato is another Italian term used to express musical ideas. The word legato literally means "to unite or bind." Legato means a smooth connection from one note to the next. Legato and slurs may seem similar, but they are different. Legato is a way to phrase notes so that they are smoothly connected. Slurs are a technique. Legato will be written as a word above the section of music you are playing.

PHRASE MARKINGS

Sometimes slur markings are used to show musical phrases. Composers do this to show the larger sense of where the phrases are. Phrase markings look identical to slur markings; they just extend much longer (see the following figure). It does not always mean that each note should be slurred—and in fact this may be impossible on your instrument. What it does mean is that you should do the best you can to connect those notes and make them sound flowing and well connected.

ARTICULATIONS OF LENGTH

The Long and the Short of It

The length of a note is typically set by the rhythm. However, special articulations such as staccato and tenuto affect the overall length of notes with their own special symbols.

STACCATO

Staccato is a marking that instructs you to play any note a bit shorter than it's written. Staccato is symbolized by a small dot that is placed directly over or under the notehead (see the next figure). The staccato dot is placed on the alternate side of the stem. If the stem faces down, place the dot above the notehead; if the stem faces up, place the dot below it.

Staccato is an inexact science. There is no rule to tell you just how short the note should be; it just means to play it shorter than it's written. Staccato is typically reserved for faster note values—usually quarters, eighths, and sixteenths. It wouldn't make much sense to have a staccato whole note! A staccato is an effective way for a composer to space out notes without having to write faster note values and rests; it's easier for players to read staccatos.

Notable

Brass and woodwind instruments produce articulations by tonguing, which is the use of the tongue to break the airflow to the instrument. Bowed string instruments use different bowing techniques to produce different articulations.

STACCATISSIMO

Staccatissimo is the more extreme version of staccato. It indicates that the note should be played as short as humanly possible. Staccatissimo has its own symbol, shown in the following figure.

Staccatissimos follow the same rules as staccato markings in terms of how and when they are placed. You will never see a staccatissimo marking on the longer notes.

TENUTO

A tenuto marking simply tells you to play a note for its full written value. A tenuto is a small flat line above or below the notehead (see the next figure).

Tenuto markings are handy when you have myriad staccato markings and one or more notes needs to be obviously longer than the rest. Sometimes placing the tenuto marking on those notes draws attention to them, more so than just removing the staccato does. Besides indicating that a note should be held for its full value, a tenuto marking typically implies that the note should have a bit more weight to it than normal. In this case, tenuto markings have more than one meaning. Markings that affect the strength and loudness of notes deserve their own heading.

ARTICULATIONS OF STRENGTH

Pump Up the Volume

Dynamics deal with larger sections of music and changes in the loudness or softness. When single notes, or selected notes, need to be played louder or softer, special symbols are used to denote changes in the strength and weight of those notes. These indicate to the player more information about how to play that note.

ACCENTS

You have learned about dynamic markings such as forte and piano. Dynamic markings change the volume of sections of music. While it's possible to mark one single note loud and the next one soft with forte and piano indications, it's impractical to do so. The accent marking—which looks like this: >—is a way for certain notes to jump out a touch (see the following figure). When you see accent markings, give those notes more stress and dynamic level than the other notes. The composer wants those notes to stand out, so give them a bit more weight and energy.

You'll see accent markings alternate on the stems—either above or below. This is consistent with the other markings you have seen in this chapter. Most extra markings go on the alternate side of the stems so they don't get in the way.

MARCATO

A marcato is akin to a superaccent (see the following figure). When you encounter marcato symbols, play those notes with great strength and great accent. Those notes should jump right out of the music. Following the trend of other musical symbols, marcato markings hover under or over the notes that they affect—always on the alternate side of the stem.

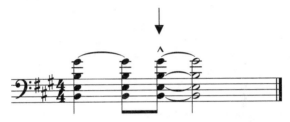

SIMILE

If any of the articulations listed in this chapter go on for a prolonged period without break, it may be more efficient for the composer to write a bar or two of the articulations and simply say simile for the rest of the music (see the following). The simile instructs you to continue the articulations until further notice.

At the point when you should stop playing those articulations, the composer manually writes out the last measure of the articulations. After that, if the composer wanted to remove those articulations, the bars would be written without them. Take a look at the next figure to see how this is done.

These notes are played without articulation

COMBINED ARTICULATIONS

Articulations can be combined; they need not be singular in purpose. You can have a staccato note with an accent. Almost any of the articulations can be combined. The next figure shows all the possible combinations of articulations.

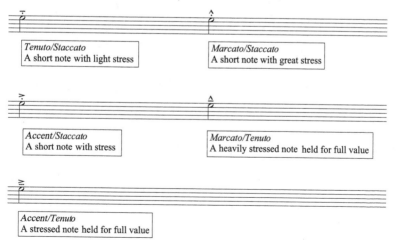

The only articulations that can't be combined are ones that mean the same thing. For example, since staccato and staccatissimo mean the same thing to varying degrees, you'll never see them combined. Also, accents and marcatos wouldn't be combined for the very same reason. Everything else can and will be combined at the discretion of the composer and the music.

PERFORMANCE INDICATIONS

How You Should Play

The next batch of musical markings are grouped under performance indications because they give you information about how to play a piece—or, how not to play. These indications are different from expression markings. They are essential, common musical symbols you will encounter.

BREATH MARKS

When playing a wind instrument or singing, the element of breathing becomes an important part of musical flow. While it's a no-brainer that you have to breathe at some point, the point at which you breathe can define the phrases. Breathing can make or break a phrase! The next figure shows what a breath mark looks like.

Notable

Not only is the breath mark a common symbol to find, but it will also aid in your own practice if you play brass or woodwinds or sing; you can mark up your own phrases to assist in performing.

CAESURA

Music doesn't always flow from measure to measure. Music is very much like water in that it ebbs and flows naturally. Music also takes pauses. One such pause is called the caesura. A caesura, which is signified as a ▰, allows music to suddenly take a brief pause. When you come across a caesura, you take a slight pause of an indeterminate length. You don't have time to get a sandwich—it's just a short point of rest. If you are playing with other players, such as in chamber groups, choirs, orchestras, or bands, caesuras need to be agreed upon. If you play with a conductor, she will usually cue everyone in together. When playing alone, you are in control of the length of a caesura.

FERMATA

A fermata is the opposite of a caesura; it extends the length of a note by an indeterminate amount. Fermatas can affect single notes or chords. You typically find fermatas at the end of sections and at the conclusion of musical phrases (see the next figure). Like caesuras, fermatas don't go on forever. The conductor, other players, or you will dictate their length.

OCTAVE SIGNS

Bumping It Up (or Down) a Notch

Since the musical alphabet only gives players seven letters to work with, the same letter names are played in different "octaves" across the music staff. Sometimes when parts reach too high on the staff and excessive ledger lines are required, they can be very difficult to read. Music has a set of symbols that allow the notes to be written in a comfortable range while indicating to the player to manually adjust the notes up or down in octaves. These markings make the player's life easier. No one likes to read notes that are too high or too low.

If the composer wishes you to play one octave higher, the music will be marked with an 8va, 8va, or all'ottava, which literally means "at the octave." An 8va marking would appear above the notes that should be played up one octave. A dotted line extends over all the notes that are to be raised up. The last note under the dotted line has either a small downward hook or the word *loco*, which means "at place," or back to normal. Let's take a look at an example before (see the first figure) and after (see the second figure) an 8va marking and you decide which you'd rather read. The 8va symbol is typically only used on treble clef parts.

The marking 8vb, which stands for ottava bassa, is used when the composer wants a part played one octave down. The 8vb sign is placed under the notes to lower them. You will only see this used on bass clefs. Its notation mirrors the 8va markings with a long outstretched dashed line extending across the affected notes (see the next two figures). The term *loco* is traditionally placed at the end of a section to remind the player to return to the normal notes as written. Again, look at the notation and decide which you'd rather read!

Notable

While it's rare, it does happen that you have to raise or lower a section by two octaves. The piano is the best example of this due to its large range in either direction. Other instruments read these markings too! The marking 15*ma*, or quindicesima, translates to "at the fifteenth," which is two octaves up. The rules for its placement are the same as 8va—the only difference is that you raise to the second octave. Likewise, 15*ma* bassa lowers a part two octaves. The same rules apply for placement as with 8vb. These are rarely seen, but they do occur from time to time.

MISCELLANEOUS SYMBOLS

Additional Accessories

There are still a few symbols that you haven't learned about yet. The rest of the symbols are hard to group together in any other way than lumping them together as miscellaneous.

TRILLS

Trills, which fall into the larger category of ornaments, are ways to dress up notes. This technique of ornamenting notes was very popular in the baroque era. A trill is a rapid alternation of a note and the next note above it (see the next figure).

As you can see, a trill is represented either by a tr and/or the **tr** symbol. All that is shown is the principal note and the trill symbol above it. The duration of the principal note determines how long the trill lasts. You rapidly alternate between the principal note and the note immediately above it as many times as you can in the time allotted. In a traditional trill, you start with the upper note. If you see a C with a trill sign above it, the trill starts on the D above. In certain periods, trills were reversed and began with the principal note, so you must be aware of when the music was written to know which is correct.

Trills have a few quirks that you need to know about. First, the upper note that you trill from is taken from the key or scale that the piece is currently in. From the original written pitch, you go up one note in the scale and alternate back and forth quickly. You can place a ♯ or a ♭ symbol either next to the trill symbol or above it to denote that the upper note is altered.

Notable

The most standard definition of a trill is to start the trill on the upper note. However, in the romantic period, trills turned around and the figure started on the principal note and trilled upward. This is the opposite of how trills were performed before this period. There is no difference in the notation of either; you just have to know the age of the piece you are playing and what was stylistically correct when it was written to know what the composer intended. For most music you trill starting with the upper note.

OSSIA MEASURES

An ossia (meaning "or else") measure is a floating alternate measure that gives you an alternate phrase of music to play. The ossia measure will be written above the measure you are playing, or below a joined grand staff. Ossia measures are used to write out trills and other difficult ornaments (see the following figure). They can also illustrate another way to play a selection of music. Simply, an ossia is an alternate measure of music that you can play instead of the normal measure.

As you can see, the ossia measure seems to hang from nowhere above the measure in question. In this case, the ossia measure spells out how the trill is to be played. You find these often in baroque music where many of the difficult ornaments need clarification. An ossia can also be used to provide an easier alternative for a difficult phrase.

TREMOLO

A tremolo is a fast set of repeating notes. String players often have to play long stretches of repeated notes. Instead of writing out each one, tremolo shorthand can be used (see the first figure). But tremolo does not always mean the same note. If you are playing a piece where two or more notes are repeated for a long time, a tremolo marking can be used as well (see the second figure).

Eighth-Note *Tremolo*
(One Slash Through the Stem)

Sixteenth-Note *Tremolo*
(Two Slashes Through the Stem)

Interval *Tremolo*

The number of slanted stems between the notes signifies the rhythm of the repeated tremolo while the rhythmic duration of the principal notes signifies the length of the tremolo. It's much easier to see a half note with a tremolo sign through its stem than to see bar after bar of identical sixteenth notes—at sixteen notes per bar, it can be very easy to get lost. Tremolos are common for string players and pianists. In theory any instrument can have them.

GLISSANDO

A glissando is something that most of us have performed on a piano. Have you ever walked up to a piano and dragged your finger across the white keys? That's a glissando. It's merely shorthand to signify that you rapidly slide through all those notes. A glissando is signified by a starting and ending note, with a long line connecting the two notes. The term *gliss* may or may not accompany the line (see the following figure).

Piano and harp glissandi easily, as it simply requires dragging your hand across the instrument. Other instruments that perform glissandos do so "chromatically," as they play every note possible between the starting and ending point. It's typically seen in piano and harp music.

Chapter 11

Applying Musical Theory Knowledge

You now have a robust working knowledge of the amazing, intricate, and specific ways that music works. You can spell chords, you can listen for harmonies, you can identify and build a scale, and you can tell what harmonies are dissonant and why. Now, let's apply that information to how you approach music: playing and listening, and even arranging and composing.

In this chapter you'll learn about the different kinds of instruments, what kind of music they make and how, and how they play together. This chapter also looks at how music has to be altered, or transposed, so that instruments in different keys can play together. That involves both intervals and moving things around the staff—in other words, music theory in action.

THE DIFFERENT TYPES OF INSTRUMENTS

Making the Band

Now that you have an understanding of how music works, we can discuss how music is played: on instruments. All the instruments in the Western world can be grouped into just a few major categories: strings, brass, winds, and percussion. All follow the same rules of music, and all read the same sheet music. But how each of these instruments work to create sound, or rather music, is quite different.

STRINGED INSTRUMENTS

Obviously, these are the instruments that have strings: violins, violas, cellos, stand-up bass, guitars, bass guitars, and pianos. Open up a piano—it's not a direct string being plucked or triggered by a bow, but keys do cause strings to vibrate, which is how a stringed instrument makes sound.

BRASS INSTRUMENTS

While they can be made of any light, moldable metal, brass is just shorthand for the instruments in a symphony or otherwise that work via a combination of air being forced through the pipes of a metal instrument, whose tone is altered with valves, keys, or a slide. For example: the trumpet, the tuba, the baritone, and the trombone.

WOODWINDS

Similar to brass instruments in that air is breathed into a series of holes that changes that air into magical musical sound, woodwinds are made of metal or wood (hence the traditional if outdated name) and filter the air through reeds. The air goes in, and keys and a series of complicated fingerings determine what notes come out. Examples of woodwinds are flutes, clarinets, and oboes.

PERCUSSION

Most percussion instruments don't provide what you would ordinarily define as melody or even an element of harmony. You can't make harmony by yourself, it's true, but drums offer quick, percussive sounds to accentuate the other music in a band or symphony while also keeping rhythm or time in a way that adds a hard-charging, forward-moving, and ultimately ear-pleasing element to the proceedings. Drums are of course percussion instruments, but in a symphony percussion instruments also include instruments that provide tones, but ones that are only capable of performing set, unchanging tones.

Notable

The triangle is a percussion instrument because it can only play one note, no matter what you do to it. The xylophone is also a percussion instrument because while it can play the whole range of notes, they can't be augmented—the keys are there, and they must be struck.

INSTRUMENT AND VOCAL RANGES

Knowing the Limits of Sound

It's been established that each instrument, or at least each instrument family, contributes differently to the orchestra. Not every instrument can play more than one note for example, and some are better at harmonizing than they are at melody. Different instrument groupings can even play the same piece of music in different clefs. One of the main differences that sets instruments apart from one another are their ranges. Knowing exactly what an instrument is capable of (or incapable of, as the case may be) can greatly inform how you select or play an instrument, or even how you write and arrange music.

The following figures show the ranges for just about every major instrument—from the very top of their possibilities down to how low they can go. (It's also helpful to know what keys certain instruments can handle.)

STRING RANGES

Here are the basic ranges for string instruments: the electric guitar, bass guitar, violin, viola, violoncello (commonly known as just cello), and string bass.

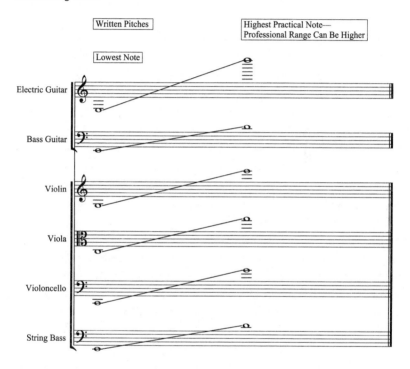

BRASS RANGES

The brass instrument group includes the French horn, trumpet, trombone, baritone horn (usually called just baritone), and tuba. The next figure shows the range for brass instruments.

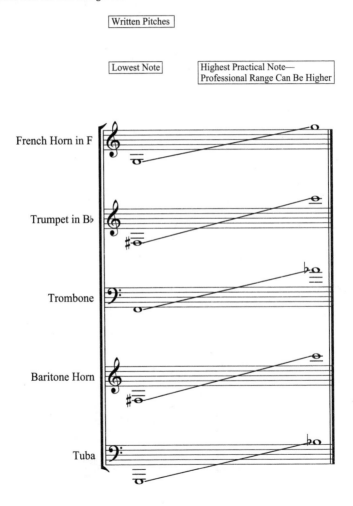

WIND RANGES

Here are woodwind instruments and their ranges. This covers the piccolo, flute, oboe, clarinet, soprano saxophone, alto saxophone, tenor saxophone, baritone saxophone, and bassoon.

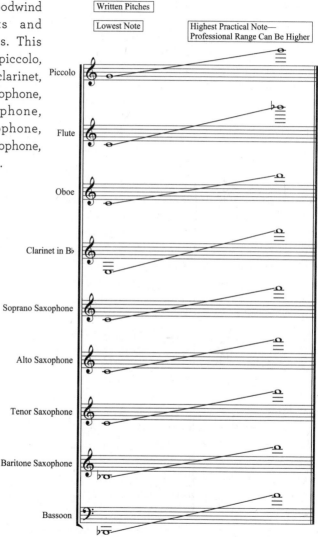

VOCAL RANGES

But what about the most prominent and commonly played instrument in the world: the human voice? People are so different and are capable of creating such a wide range of pitches with their mouths, throats, diaphragms, and air that there are a handful of different vocal ranges into which singers' voices can be categorized.

- **Bass:** The name comes from the Latin *bassus*, which means "low" or "short." It's the lowest vocal range possible, and bass singers provide rich and deep tones. Bass voices are almost universally male.
- **Baritone:** It means "deep sounding," although this male voice is slightly higher than a bass voice. In classical, there are two baritone styles: lyric baritone, which focuses on the higher end of the range, and the dramatic baritone, which brings up the bottom.
- **Tenor:** It's the second-highest male singing voice (second only to the relatively rare countertenor), and the name comes from the Latin word *tenere*, or "to hold." That's because tenors traditionally were responsible for or "held" the main melody.
- **Alto:** That's Italian for "high," so you can guess what kind of voices are alto: high, female ones.
- **Mezzo-soprano:** "Middle soprano" singers have a higher range than an alto, but not as high as a soprano.
- **Soprano:** The highest, lightest, and brightest classical female singing voice, it gets its name from *supra*, Latin for "above."
- **Falsetto:** The notes these high-singing male voices may deliver are indeed higher than those from a tenor or countertenor, but the name says it all—*falsetto* means "false." Falsetto singers perform in an artificially high voice and don't really use regular singing technique to reach the high end of their natural register.

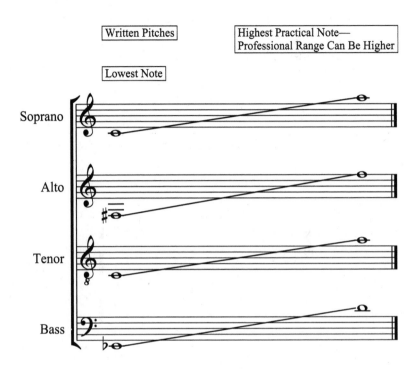

Notable

Here are some famous examples for each for each of those vocal ranges and techniques. Bass: R&B star Barry White. Baritone: country singer Johnny Cash. Tenor: legendary opera singer Enrico Caruso. Alto: Adele. Mezzo-soprano: Aretha Franklin. Soprano: Maria Callas. Falsetto: the Bee Gees.

TRANSPOSING MUSIC

Translating for Instruments in Different Keys

One of the most potentially nerve-wracking ways to apply music theory to real-life musical purposes is the act of transposing instruments, or converting music across keys, ranges, and instrumental capabilities. It's certainly detail-oriented and time-consuming work, but when you learn about the different instruments (and their different keys) and how to transpose their music, you also learn about range, composition, and arranging along the way.

A symphonic score—the one a conductor uses—is arranged for multiple instruments. It's a complicated document for a novice to read, but it demonstrates the importance of transposing: different instruments naturally play in different keys. The alto saxophone and clarinet, while both in the woodwind family, actually can't play off of the same formatted sheet music. One instrument's music would have to be translated, or transposed, so that the other instrument could use it.

CONCERT PITCH

On a scientific level, notes exist as vibrations of air. The speed at which they vibrate can be measured and is expressed in hertz (Hz). The only true measure of a note is its frequency in hertz. A large group of instruments plays in concert pitch, meaning that when they play or read a note on the musical staff, they are getting the mathematically correct answer. When a piano plays a middle C, it's playing a note with a frequency of 261 Hz—it's an exact thing; the piano is playing concert pitch. Other instruments play at concert pitch, and they're known as C instruments.

The most common include:

- Violin
- Viola
- Cello
- Harp
- Guitar

- Flute
- Oboe
- Bassoon
- Trombone
- Tuba

Guitar and bass guitar do as well, but with the notable quirk of having music knocked down an octave so their music stays within the staff, but that's still considered concert pitch. (Another thing that sounds at concert pitch is an orchestral tuning note. When a symphony tunes up, the oboe player rings a concert A note, and the rest of the orchestra tunes to get as close to this note as possible.)

Notable

A great example of concert pitch is an orchestral tuning note. When a symphony orchestra tunes up, the oboe player plays a concert A note and the rest of the orchestra tunes up to this note. Most tuning forks that provide a tuning pitch also provide the same concert A (A = 440 Hz).

Meanwhile, the common instruments that do (and often have to) transpose are:

- Clarinet
- French horn
- Trumpet
- Saxophone—soprano, alto, tenor, and baritone

HOW TRANSPOSING WORKS

A transposing instrument reads the same music as other instruments. The only difference is that when a tenor sax plays a written C, the note that comes out would not register as a C on a tuner or match a C on a piano. An entirely different note comes out! A concert B♭ is heard when a trumpet plays a written C—this is what is meant by transposition. If the following example melody for the tenor sax from the top staff was played, what comes out is actually from the bottom staff.

There are two possible reasons why some instruments transpose and others don't. The first is history. Brass instruments rely heavily on the overtone series to make their notes happen. Brass instruments used to add crooks, which were additional pipes, to play in different keys. In time, as the instruments evolved and valves became standard on brass instruments, those additional crooks were no longer necessary. Certain instruments evolved into certain keys and just stayed there. It's now been so long and there has been so much music written that it would be too difficult to change it all—either the music or the instruments.

The second reason is best shown in the saxophone family. There are four saxophones in common use today: soprano, alto, tenor, and baritone. Each of the four saxophones transposes, but differently. The reason that it's done this way has less to do with history and more to do with the ease of the player. Each of the four saxophones, while physically differing in size, has the exact same system of keys that Adolphe Sax invented in the 1800s. The sax transposes four different ways so that any sax player trained on any one of the instruments could play any of the saxophones without having to relearn anything. Each saxophone reads the same treble clef melody, and the composer makes sure that each part is transposed correctly on paper for the proper sonic result.

TRANSPOSING SHORTCUTS

For too many years, students have been generally confused as to how to transpose correctly for instruments. But there are ways to get it right. For instance, each major instrument carries with it a seldom-used key name. The trumpet should technically be known as a B♭ trumpet, but nobody calls it that. However, knowing those full names provides clues as to how they transpose. The other is this little nugget of easily memorized information: an instrument's key name is the note heard in concert pitch when that instrument plays its written C.

Let's put this to work with the trumpet, or rather B♭ trumpet, since the instrument has a key of B♭. Recalling that line about concert pitch: B♭ is the note heard—in concert pitch—when the trumpet plays a written C.

This means that whatever note is written for trumpet will come out exactly one whole step below what is written. So what can composers do to fix this? They simply write the trumpet part *up* a whole step, in a written D. The trumpet player will read and play the D, yet a perfect C will come out in concert key. Sounding down and writing up is the case for most transposing instruments.

TRANSPOSING E♭ INSTRUMENTS

Two common instruments lay in the key of E♭: the E♭ alto saxophone and the E♭ baritone saxophone. Being in the key of E♭ means that when these instruments read a written C, an E♭ concert pitch is heard. The E♭ alto saxophone transposes a major sixth away from where it's written. In this case, a melody written in concert pitch would have to be transposed up a major sixth to sound right on the alto saxophone.

The baritone saxophone is also in the key of E. But as it naturally resides a full octave below the alto sax, it transposes at the intervals of a major sixth and an octave (also known as a major thirteenth). For a melody written in concert key to sound correctly on a baritone sax, it must be written up a major.

TRANSPOSING F INSTRUMENTS

Just two instruments transpose in the key of F: the French horn and the English horn. Both the French horn and the English horn (also called a tenor oboe) transpose the same: a fifth away. If a composer writes a melody in concert key and wants the French horn and English horn to play correctly, he must write the melody up a perfect fifth for it to work.

TRAINING YOUR EAR

Recognizing Musical Elements

Now you've learned about all the individual elements and systems that combine to create complex musical harmonies, melodies, and chords. You have everything you need to apply that knowledge to the music in the world around you. Use your ears *and* your newly acquired musical perception abilities—such as relative pitch—as well as some examples so you know what to look for when you hear music.

LISTENING FOR INTERVALS

One way that you can accelerate your music theory ability is to use your ears: relate intervals to famous songs. See Chapter 2 for a list of common intervals and the songs they relate to.

IDENTIFYING CHORDS

Major chords just kind of sound bright and happy, a perception reinforced by movie scores and pop music. Passages of triumph in the former are almost always in a major key, for example, and so are pop songs about love. Conversely, because of their slightly unsettling feel, minor chords have carried with them the baggage of sadness, foreboding, and mystery.

Notable

"The Imperial March" from John Williams's iconic Star Wars score (the Darth Vader music) is in a minor key; so is the curious, tentative beginning of Beethoven's ultimately delightful "Moonlight" Sonata.

Diminished chords are a bit harder to identify—if only because they're less common and generally don't surround major melodies. But they can be found in film scores, underscoring tense or suspenseful situations. Diminished chords are likewise the go-to music in soap operas and in those old movies when the bad guy is tying a woman to the railroad tracks as a train approaches.

WHAT AM I LISTENING TO?

Different Types of Musical Compositions

As you play more and more music—or at least analyze more and more sheet music—you'll notice that classical pieces, or symphonic and vocal compositions, are usually headlined with very technically oriented names. "Occasional Oratorio," for example or simply "Etude." These are signifiers to musicians about not only the style in which the music is to be played, but also the origins and history of that particular form, and the composer's intent in writing the piece. Here are the characteristics of but a few of the more common styles.

- **Toccata:** A loosely written piece intended to be heavily improvised and improved upon by a skilled instrumentalist, usually on a piano's keyboard or plucked strings. The name is from the Italian word *toccare*, which means "to touch." A famous example is (at least part of) Bach's Toccata and Fugue in D Minor.
- **Fugue:** A style in which two or more voices or instruments keep returning to a specific musical theme over three sections: an exposition, a development, and a final section that returns to the opening part's statement of the musical theme.
- **Etude:** This is one of the rare musical words that's French, not Italian—it means "to study." An etude is a short, difficult-to-play piece designed to train a musician to play faster and better, but when performed is quite impressive. (Chopin published several sets of etudes in the 1830s.)
- **Ode:** A simple, often short celebratory composition written in praise of a subject. Beethoven's "Ode to Joy," for example.
- **Sonata:** A piece meant to feature an individual instrumental soloist, but often with a piano or harpsichord accompaniment. (Or just the piano or harpsichord.) A sonata is traditionally arranged into four movements: an allegro (a brief, fast-moving introduction), then

a slow section, a dance movement, and a rapid finale. (The most famous sonata is probably Beethoven's "Moonlight" Sonata.)

- **Oratorio:** It's very similar to an opera in that it's a large composition for a full orchestra and multiple singers, including soloists who deliver arias. The difference is that an opera is a piece of fully realized theater, with costumes and sets. An oratorio does have a plot and characters and all the action is fully sung, but is presented as a concert by singers standing on a stage. (Probably the most famous oratorio is Handel's *Messiah*, composed in 1741.)

- **Aria:** A self-contained song within the whole of an opera or oratorio. It's essentially a solo, but can be performed with or without the backing of instruments. (One aria used often in movies is "Habanera" from Bizet's 1875 opera *Carmen*.)

- **Divertimento:** A jaunty, short, light-hearted instrumental piece written for a small ensemble. (Mozart wrote a lot of these.)

- **Canon:** A piece in which a strong melody is presented boldly up front, and then other instruments or voices join in to repeat that melody, but changed in some way, such as with a different rhythm or chord structure. (Probably the most famous canon is Pachelbel's Canon in D. Canons in which all the repetitions are exactly the same are called rounds—such as "Row, Row, Row Your Boat.")

- **Intermezzo:** Translating roughly to "in the middle," this is a composition that was written to fill space between acts of a play, for example, or as a transitory bridge between movements of a symphony or other long work of music.

Notable

There are two essential kinds of intermezzo: the opera intermezzo and the instrumental intermezzo. The opera intermezzo is a comedic interlude between acts of an opera. This type usually features slapstick comedy, disguises, and dialect. The instrumental intermezzo was a movement between two others in a larger work, or even a character piece that could stand on its own.

Final Exam

Analyzing a Piece of Music

Congratulations: You've made it through music theory "boot camp." You've learned to notice chords, melody, and harmony, how intervals and progressions work, and how they're all used together to craft beautiful music for the ages. Now, let's apply some of what you learned and take a deep look at one example of that beautiful music: Beethoven's Ninth Symphony.

The Symphony No. 9 in D Minor (completed in 1824) is Beethoven's final complete symphony and perhaps the most recognizable work of classical music. It was also the first example of a major composer using voices in a symphony. It is considerd by many critics to be Beethoven's greatest work and one of the best compositions in the Western musical cannon.

INSTRUMENTATION

Say you were to get your hands on a complete sheet music version of the symphony, the kind from which a conductor would use to conduct. Among the first things included would be a list of instruments Beethoven has required for his piece to be performed the way he intended it to be performed. The Ninth Symphony calls for:

- Piccolo
- Flute
- Oboe
- Clarinets (in B♭, C, and A)
- Bassoon
- Contrabassoon
- French horns (in D, E♭, B♭, and even bass B♭)

- Trumpet (in both B♭ and D)
- Trombones
- Percussion (including timpani)
- Violin
- Viola
- Cello
- Bass
- A four-part choir

TRANSPOSING THE MUSIC

In order for a conductor (or in this case, you, playing conductor) to know what she wants out of her orchestra, she has to know what each member of the orchestra is playing. And that means transposing their parts into concert pitch.

The easiest way to do this, at least for the sake of this exercise, is to pick out a few single chords from a part of the symphony—such as the fourth movement. (It also happens to contain "Ode to Joy.") Let's look at two measures in the key of D minor.

While all the instruments are listed upfront, Beethoven didn't use all of them all at the same time throughout the symphony. The following section for instance features the flute, oboe, clarinet, bassoon, contrabassoon, horn in D, horn in B, trumpet in D, trombone, violin, viola, cello, and bass.

So, first you need to figure out which instruments are already in concert key and which ones need to be transposed. This is easy: in the instrument list, an instrument that isn't in concert pitch already is listed as such—Bb clarinet, and so forth. That whittles down the task to merely Bb clarinet, horn in D, and trumpet in D.

Now, go over their transpositions individually to bring them all into concert pitch in their own way.

- For Bb clarinet, transpose the notes down a whole step.
- For the horn in D, transpose the notes *up* a whole step.
- For trumpet in D, do what you did to the horn in D: transpose it up a whole step.

Here's what those notes will look like in concert pitch.

Now, insert them back into the score and in concert pitch so you can continue your analysis.

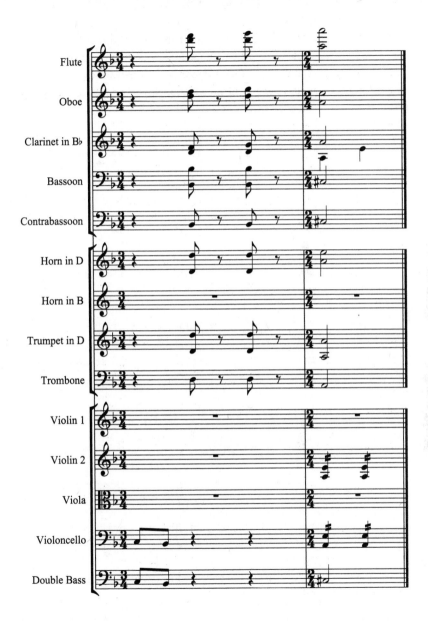

CHORD CONSTRUCTION AND ANALYSIS

Now that you've (almost) literally got all the instruments on the same page, you can start looking at how they come together to play chords. The roots can come from the lowest tones, which here would be provided by the lowest instruments on the piece: the bass and contrabassoon. But look what chords emerged (see next image).

Those are triads: B♭, G minor, and A triads, to be exact. Because even though a symphony is long and complex (or just one movement) and involves so many instruments, there aren't all that many notes. Beethoven was a tonal composer who relied heavily on triads and seventh chords; his symphonies take a three-note chord and voice it throughout a huge orchestra, doubling notes where necessary to create a monster, cohesive sound. The foundations of harmony simply don't change in the scientific world of music.

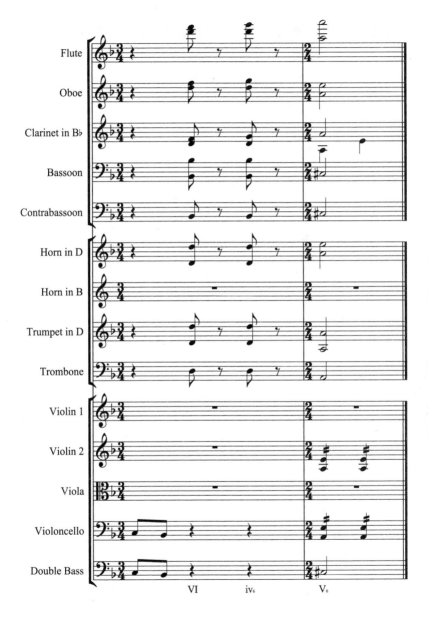

INDEX